Deep Frying
for
All Seasons

Over 125 Great Recipes for
Delicious Deep-Fried Foods!

Debra Marie Thomas

Pascoe Publishing, Inc.
Rocklin, California

Cover design by Knockout Books
Page Design by Melanie Haage Design

Published in the United States of America by
Pascoe Publishing, Inc.
Rocklin, California
http://www.pascoepublishing.com

ISBN: 1-929862-18-0

04   05   10   9   8   7   6   5   4

Printed in the United States of America

Table of Contents

Chapter One: Introduction

Chapter Two: Great Beginnings — Appetizers & Snacks

Chapter Three: Warm Breakfast Delights

Chapter Four: Homestyle Entrée Favorites

Chapter Five: Vegetables & Side Dishes

Chapter Six: Specialties From Around the World

Chapter Seven: Breads, Hush Puppies & More

Chapter Eight: Delectable Desserts

Welcome to the world of deep-frying!

Among the extensive line of Ultrex® products, the deep fryer is one of the most exciting and versatile. My wife, Maryann, and I have enjoyed using the great recipes in *Deep Frying for All Seasons* to create everything from appetizers to main dishes and desserts. We have included some of our personal "favorite" recipes and we hope that you will enjoy them as much as we do.

We invite you to explore the entire Ultrex product line which includes cookware, appliances, bake ware and accessories. Check back with us regularly as we are always adding new products that add convenience and enjoyment to your cooking experience!

Sincerely,
Art & Maryann Krull

PS. If you are looking for some great Ultrex® pieces to add to your collection, please visit us at: www.hsn.com. Keyword "Ultrex."

CHAPTER ONE

Introduction

Great cooking doesn't begin and end with a single kitchen appliance, but a single appliance can make the difference between an ordinary meal and a truly memorable one. Such is the case with today's new deep fryer found in family kitchens around the world.

Today's deep fryers have the capacity to make your meals exciting and absolutely fun. Why? The fryers have key safety features. Many have odor-removing filters. Unlike fryers of years past, today's fryers close completely and often lock, eliminating oil splatters and drips all over the kitchen. In short, today's deep fryers are safe, versatile and convenient!

The recipes in this book have been created to accompany today's fryers. We all love deep-fried classics—fried chicken, French fries, fritters and onion rings. But, we can also add so many new taste sensations—international favorites, deep-fried vegetables of all kinds and sophisticated salads. Many recipes in this book are delicious accompaniments or gourmet additions for special occasions. Whether you use your deep fryer to create an entrée for guests or to whip up a few snacks for the kids, you'll find that your deep fryer is a great companion for any occasion.

DEEP FRYING HINTS:

◇ Deep frying allows food to quickly form a crisp, brown crust. This locks in the moisture of the food and enhances the natural flavor of the food. Frying at the proper temperature is critical to the success of your foods. Foods fried in temperatures that are too low will be soggy and heavy with oil. Foods fried in temperatures that are too high will result in burned crusts or exterior areas and uncooked ingredients in the middle.

◇ Deep fryers vary in several features, depending on the model and manufacturer of each. Carefully refer to your manufacturer's instructions when using your deep fryer and be aware of the specific cautions mentioned.

◇ Because deep-frying involves cooking with oil heated to very high temperatures, it is important to be attentive to the frying process. Deep-frying requires only a few minutes for most foods, so it's important to be present while food is cooking or any time the fryer is heating up or cooling down. Do not leave your fryer unattended, particularly if children are nearby.

◇ The oil used for frying is critical to the success of your efforts. Most oils will begin to break down when exposed to very high heat for sustained periods of time, which then tempers the flavoring of the food negatively. Oil or shortening will smoke when they begin to break down, so be observant to any signs of smoke. Vegetable oil, soybean oil and solid shortening are best when used at temperatures under 370°F. When cooking at the highest heat, use peanut oil for the best results. Peanut oil can be heated to 400°F and offers superior flavor and versatility for deep frying foods. Although it is more expensive, it is recommended for best results.

◇ Properly maintaining the oil you use for deep-frying will directly affect your foods. You should strain the oil after each use and replace it after using it 4-5 times. If you fry fish or other distinctive foods, you should replace the oil immediately.

◇ Discard the oil by first allowing it to cool in the fryer. Drain the fryer according to the manufacturer's instructions and place in an empty coffee can or other receptacle that will safely hold the oil. The oil should be completely cool before covering. Cover the oil with an airtight cover. Do not put hot oil in a garbage can or plastic container.

◇ Although fires caused by overheated oil or shortening are rare, they should always be smothered using baking soda, towels or salt. When frying, place one of these items nearby as a precaution. Do not attempt to put water on any burning oil, as this will only cause the fire to spread.

◇ Most fried foods are battered or coated in some fashion. This allows the food inside to remain tender, while the outer layer is cooked to a crisp perfection. Several recipes in this book call for batters or coatings and they may be interchanged, depending on the food used with the coating.

◇ The most important aspect of using a batter or coating is to prevent the excess on any piece of food from dropping into the oil. Allow any excess batter or coating to drip off before placing foods in the fryer. This keeps the oil clean and at the proper temperature.

◇ The temperature in your deep fryer will fall as soon as food is placed in it. Because the proper temperature must be maintained for good results, it is especially important to fry only a few pieces of food at a time. Smaller foods, such as croutons or hush puppies, can be fried in greater quantities at the same time. However, larger pieces of food, such as bone-in chicken, fish or whole onions, require more space and should be fried alone or with only 1-2 additional pieces at the same time. Overcrowding the fryer is one of the most common reasons for unsuccessful results.

◇ Most foods should be as dry as possible when placed in the deep fryer. Foods that are wet will typically cause the coating or batter to slide off and will not fry to a crisp crust.

CHAPTER TWO

Great Beginnings: Appetizers & Snacks

There's something about the anticipation of an exciting meal just minutes or hours away. Appetizers are intended to be exactly that—a little bit of something delicious to whet your appetite for the meal to follow. The recipes in this chapter offer a wide variety of appetizer choices, from *Super Crispy Potato Skins* and *Crispy Browned Bananas with Lemon Aioli* to *Cajun Onion Blossoms* and *Smoked Salmon & Cream Cheese Wontons*. Choose a different appetizer recipe for every night of the week and get ready for a great beginning!

Snacks are the mainstay of busy people with demanding schedules. With the ease of today's deep fryers, you can quickly and easily prepare *Mini Mexican Tostadas* or *Crab & Pepper Jack Quesadillas* to accent your day. Delicious snacks are just a few minutes away any time of day with the recipes inside this chapter.

Napa Valley Egg Rolls

2 12 oz. jars marinated
artichokes, drained

8 oz. cream cheese, softened

1 egg, beaten

2 green onions, minced

1 t. garlic, minced

salt and pepper to taste

12 egg roll wrappers

oil for frying

 Use a blender or food processor to blend together the 1 jar of the artichokes, the cream cheese and the egg. Remove the mixture with a spatula and place in a medium bowl. Roughly chop the remaining jar of artichokes and add to the blended mixture. Add the onions, garlic, salt and pepper and mix lightly.

To form the egg rolls, place 1 wrapper on a clean surface or dinner plate. Add 1 heaping tablespoon of the artichoke and cheese filling. Tuck in each end and wrap tightly lengthwise. Lightly moisten a fingertip with water and seal the edge of the egg roll wrapper. Heat the deep fryer to 375°F according to the manufacturer's instructions. Place 4-6 egg rolls in the oil and fry for 3 minutes or until the egg rolls are crispy and browned. Drain the rolls on absorbent paper and repeat the process with the remaining rolls.

Crispy Browned Bananas with Lemon Aioli

4 unripe bananas (slightly green and firm)
salt and pepper to taste
oil for frying

Lemon Aioli:
1 T. fresh lemon juice
4 T. mayonnaise
pinch salt

 Peel the bananas and cut into 2-inch rounds. The bananas should be firm without any mushiness. Heat the deep fryer to 340°F according to the manufacturer's instructions. Place 6-8 banana rounds into the oil and fry for approximately 2 minutes. The banana rounds should be lightly browned when done. Remove the bananas to drain on absorbent paper and sprinkle lightly with the salt and pepper. Repeat the process with the remaining bananas. In a small serving bowl, combine the lemon, mayonnaise and salt. Serve the warm banana rounds with the *Lemon Aioli*. Serves 6-8.

Crab & Fresh Herb Appetizers

1/2 lb. crab meat, fresh or canned	2 T. prepared cocktail sauce
1 1/2 c. soft bread crumbs	1 t. Worcestershire sauce
1 egg, beaten	1/2 t. prepared mustard
1 T. fresh parsley, minced	salt and pepper to taste
2 T. fresh green onion, minced	1 c. saltine crackers, finely crushed
1 t. fresh cilantro, minced	oil for frying

Combine the crab meat, bread crumbs and egg in a large bowl. Lightly toss with a fork. Add the parsley, green onion and cilantro and toss again. Add the cocktail sauce, Worcestershire sauce, mustard, salt and pepper and toss again. Cover and chill in the refrigerator for 1 hour. To assemble, form the crab mixture into 36 balls, each about the size of a small walnut. Roll each in the crushed saltine crackers. Set aside.

Heat the deep fryer to 355°F according to the manufacturer's instructions. Place 6 to 8 crab appetizers into the hot oil. Fry for 3-4 minutes each until lightly browned. Remove the cooked appetizers to drain on absorbent paper and repeat the process with the remaining balls. Serve hot. Serves 12.

Mini Mexican Tostadas

1 lb. lean ground beef, cooked and drained

1 t. ground chili powder

1/2 t. black pepper

1/2 t. salt

1 medium onion, minced finely

12 small corn tortillas

16 oz. can black beans, drained

8 oz. can corn, drained

1 c. fresh green lettuce, finely shredded

1 c. Jack cheese, shredded

oil for frying

In a large bowl, mix together the ground beef, chili powder, pepper, salt and onion. With a 3-inch cookie cutter, cut rounds from each corn tortilla. Save the remaining pieces of the tortillas to fry for chips. Heat the deep fryer to 375°F according to the manufacturer's instructions. Place 3 tortilla rounds in the deep fryer. Fry for 2-3 minutes, or until each tortilla is crispy and lightly browned. Drain the shells on absorbent paper. Repeat with the remaining shells.

To assemble the mini tostadas, layer on top of each shell, 1 heaping tablespoon of the beef mixture, 1 tablespoon of black beans and 1 tablespoon of corn. Scatter a bit of lettuce over the corn and sprinkle cheese over all. Serve immediately. Serves 12-14.

Fresh Asparagus Roll-Ups

2 lbs. fresh thin asparagus, woody
   stems removed

1 c. mayonnaise

1/4 c. Parmesan cheese, finely
   shredded

1/2 t. salt

1 t. black pepper

1 loaf soft white bread, sliced,
   crusts removed

oil for frying

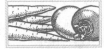 Steam the asparagus over boiling water for 6 minutes. Remove from the steamer, cool each piece and pat dry. In a small bowl, mix together the mayonnaise, cheese, salt and black pepper. To assemble, place 1 piece of bread on a clean surface and top with 1 tablespoon of the mayonnaise mixture. Place 1 piece of asparagus in the middle of the slice and roll the bread slice around the asparagus. Secure the bread with a toothpick. Repeat with the remaining bread slices and asparagus.

Heat the deep fryer to 340°F according to the manufacturer's instructions. Place 2-3 roll-ups in the fryer and fry for 3 minutes. When done, the roll-ups should be golden brown and crispy. Drain on absorbent paper and repeat the process with the remaining roll-ups. Serves 15.

Stuffed Button Mushrooms

8 oz. cream cheese, softened

1 small white onion, finely minced

2 T. garlic, finely minced

6 slices bacon, cooked and crumbled

24 large button mushrooms, cleaned, stems removed

2 eggs, beaten

2 c. saltine crackers, finely crushed

oil for frying

 In a small bowl, combine the cream cheese, onion and garlic. Mix in the crumbled bacon. Pack 1 teaspoon of the cream cheese mixture on top of each button mushroom. Dip each stuffed mushroom in the eggs and roll in the saltine cracker crumbs. Heat the deep fryer to 375°F according to the manufacturer's instructions. Place 6-8 mushrooms in the oil and fry until crispy and browned. Remove the mushrooms and drain on absorbent paper. Repeat with the remaining mushrooms. Serves 24.

Classic Chinese Egg Rolls

1 lb. ground pork	1/2 c. fresh bean sprouts, cleaned and chopped into 1-inch pieces
1 medium white onion, finely minced	
	2 T. water
1 T. vegetable oil	2 T. soy sauce
1/2 c. mushrooms, finely minced	1 t. ground ginger
2 c. fresh cabbage, finely shredded	12 egg roll wrappers
2 t. cornstarch	oil for frying

 In a large sauté pan, combine the pork, onion and oil. Cook until the pork is brown and cooked through. Drain the oil from the pork and onion. Add the mushrooms, cabbage and bean sprouts to the pan and sauté for 1 minute. In a small bowl, dissolve the cornstarch in the water and add the soy sauce and ginger. Add to the pork and vegetables and bring to a boil. Cook for 2 minutes, stirring constantly. Remove from the heat and cool.

To assemble, place 1 egg roll wrapper on a clean surface. Place 1 heaping tablespoon of the pork and vegetables in the middle, tuck in the top and bottom ends and roll completely. Lightly moisten a fingertip with water and seal the edges of the egg roll. Repeat with the remaining wrappers. Heat the deep fryer to 375°F according to the manufacturer's instructions. Place 3 egg rolls in the deep fryer and fry for 3-4 minutes, or until brown and crispy. Remove from the fryer and drain on absorbent paper. Repeat with the remaining rolls. Serve hot with additional soy sauce. Serves 12.

Deep-Fried Oysters

12 oysters
1 c. flour
1 egg, beaten

1 1/2 c. seasoned bread crumbs
oil for frying

 Heat the deep fryer to 355°F according to the manufacturer's instructions. Roll each oyster in the flour, dip in the egg, and roll in the bread crumbs. Fry 3-5 oysters at a time for 3-4 minutes, or until crispy and brown. Drain on absorbent paper and repeat with the remaining oysters. Serve immediately.

Super Crispy Potato Skins

6 medium Russet potatoes
2 c. dairy sour cream
3 T. fresh green onions, chopped

10 slices bacon, cooked and crumbled
oil for frying

 Clean and scrub the potatoes. Prick each potato with a knife or fork. Heat the oven to 400°F and bake the potatoes for 1 hour. Cool. Cut each potato in half lengthwise and scoop the potato out, leaving a shell of potato about ¼-inch thick. Reserve the potatoes for another use. Cut each potato skin into thirds lengthwise. Heat the deep fryer to 375°F according to the manufacturer's instructions. Place 4 to 6 potato skins in the deep fryer and fry for 2-3 minutes. Remove and drain each piece on absorbent paper. Repeat with the remaining potatoes.

To assemble, place the fried potato skins on a large serving platter. Top each piece with a small dollop of sour cream, a sprinkling of green onions and a few bacon bits scattered over all. Serve while warm. Makes 36 pieces.

Cheddar-Wrapped Green Olives

1 c. flour

1/2 t. cayenne pepper

1/4 c. butter or margarine, softened

1 egg, beaten

1 1/2 c. cheddar cheese, finely grated

36 pimento-stuffed green olives, drained and dried

oil for frying

 In a medium bowl, combine the flour, pepper, butter, cheddar cheese and egg. Mix thoroughly until smooth. Using a tablespoon, scoop the cheese mixture from the bowl and place a green olive inside. Wrap the cheese around the olive completely. Repeat with the remaining olives. Heat the deep fryer to 375°F according to the manufacturer's instructions. Place 8-10 cheddar-wrapped olives in the fryer and fry for 2-3 minutes. Remove the olives with a slotted spoon and drain on absorbent paper. Serve hot. Makes 36.

Crab & Pepper Jack Quesadillas

1 lb. lump crabmeat, drained and flaked

1 T. garlic, finely minced

1/4 c. white onion, finely minced

1/2 c. mayonnaise

1 t. salt

1/2 t. black pepper

1 c. pepper Jack cheese, shredded

12 8-inch flour tortillas

2 eggs, beaten

oil for frying

 In a medium bowl, combine the crab-meat, garlic, onion, mayonnaise, salt and pepper. Soften the tortillas in the microwave oven for 30 seconds. Spread approximately 3 tablespoons of the crab filling over one-half of one tortilla. Sprinkle the cheese over the crab and fold the quesadilla. Cut the quesadilla in half. Using the egg, lightly moisten all edges of each portion and seal. Repeat with the remaining tortillas.

Heat the deep fryer to 375°F according to the manufacturer's instructions. Place 3 to 4 quesadillas in the fryer and fry for 2-3 minutes, or until each is lightly browned. Remove and drain on absorbent paper. Repeat with the remaining quesadillas. Makes 48 quesadillas.

Paprika Tofu Squares

1 c. flour

1/2 t. ground Italian seasoning

1/2 t. salt

1/2 t. black pepper

1/2 t. paprika

1/2 lb. firm tofu, cut into 1-inch squares

1 egg, beaten, in a small bowl

1 c. prepared sweet and sour sauce

 In a medium bowl, combine the flour, Italian seasoning, salt, pepper and paprika. Dip each tofu square into the egg and then roll in the flour and seasonings. Heat the deep fryer to 375°F according to the manufacturer's instructions. Place 8-10 pieces of tofu in the fryer and fry until lightly browned and crispy. Remove and drain on absorbent paper. Repeat the process with the remaining tofu and seasonings. Serve warm with the sweet and sour sauce. Serves 8.

Savory Meatballs

Meatballs:
2 lbs. ground beef (use lean, if preferred)
1 egg, beaten
1/4 c. seasoned dry bread crumbs
1 clove garlic, minced
1 t. salt
1/2 t. black pepper

1/2 t. oregano
oil for frying

Meatball Coating:
1 c. prepared baking mix
1/2 c. beef broth
1 egg
1 T. dried parsley

 In a large bowl, combine the beef, egg, bread crumbs, garlic, salt, pepper and oregano. Mix lightly with your fingertips (do not over-mix as this will result in a tough texture). Form 36 small balls with the meat mixture. Prepare the meatball coating by mixing together the baking mix, broth, egg and parsley.

Heat the deep fryer to 340°F according to the manufacturer's instructions. Dip 5 or 6 meatballs in the coating and place in the fryer. Fry, turning once, until the meatballs are cooked through and browned, about 5-7 minutes. Place on a warm platter and repeat with the remaining meatballs. Serve hot. Makes 36 meatballs.

Appetizer Cheese Rounds

5 oz. process American cheese spread

1/2 c. prepared dry baking mix

1/2 t. ground chili powder

oil for frying

 In a small bowl, combine the process cheese spread and baking mix. Blend thoroughly with an electric mixer. Shape into cylinder about 1-inch in width. Sprinkle the chili powder evenly over a dinner plate. Roll the cylinder in the chili powder to cover. Cover the dough completely with plastic wrap. Place in a plastic bag and seal. Refrigerate for at least 2 hours.

Heat the deep fryer to 340°F according to the manufacturer's instructions. Cut the cheese dough into ¼-inch slices. Place the cheese rounds in the deep fryer and cook for 3-4 minutes or until lightly browned and crispy. Remove and drain on absorbent paper. Repeat with the remaining rounds. Makes about 24 slices.

Cheese & Bacon Wontons

8 oz. medium cheddar cheese, shredded

1/4 c. cream cheese, softened

1 egg, beaten

10 slices bacon, cooked and crumbled

10 wonton wrappers

oil for frying

 In a medium bowl, combine the cheddar cheese, cream cheese, egg and bacon. Mix well to blend. To assemble, place 1 heaping tablespoon of cheese filling on 1 side of 1 wonton wrapper and fold to make a triangle. Seal the edges of the wonton by lightly moistening a finger with water and running it along the edges of the wonton.

Heat the deep fryer to 375°F according to the manufacturer's instructions. Place 5-6 wonton in the fryer and fry for 5-6 minutes, or until browned and crispy. Repeat with the remaining wonton. Serves 10.

Shrimpin' Hush Puppies

1 lb. fresh shrimp, deveined, cleaned and minced

1/4 c. flour

1 egg, beaten

1/4 c. water chestnuts, finely minced

1/4 c. bamboo shoots, finely minced

1 t. salt

1/2 t. black pepper

1/2 t. fresh ginger, finely minced

1 t. fresh parsley, finely minced

2 t. cornstarch

1 T. water

oil for frying

 In a large bowl, combine the shrimp, flour, egg, water chestnuts, bamboo shoots, salt, pepper, ginger and parsley. Mix the cornstarch with the water in a small bowl and add to the shrimp mixture. Shape the shrimp into small walnut-sized balls.

Heat the deep fryer to 340°F. Place 6-8 balls in the deep fryer and fry for 4-6 minutes, or until cooked through and golden brown. Repeat with the remaining balls. Serve hot with cocktail sauce. Makes about 18 balls.

Home-Fried Tortilla Chips

12 large corn tortillas   salt to taste
oil for frying

 Cut each tortilla in half. Cut each half into thirds. Heat the deep fryer to 375°F according to the manufacturer's instructions. Place 6 tortilla chips in the fryer and fry until brown and crispy, about 5 minutes. Remove from the fryer and drain on absorbent paper. Sprinkle with salt to taste. Repeat with the remaining chips. Serve hot or store in an airtight plastic bag. Makes 72 chips.

Cajun Onion Blossoms

2 large Vidalia onions (or other sweet variety)
1 1/4 c. flour
1 t. Cajun seasoning
1 c. milk
oil for frying

Cajun Dip:
1 c. dairy sour cream
1 t. ground chili powder
1 t. Cajun seasoning

 Remove the outer skins from the onions and cut a thin slice from each top. Cut each onion, top to bottom, into fourths without cutting completely through, leaving ½-inch at the bottom. Cut each slice in half again, top to bottom, as cut previously. Cut each slice in half again as before. Continue cutting until the onion slices are as thin as possible. Open the onion slightly, using your fingertips to pull the slices apart. Place the flour and 1 teaspoon of Cajun seasoning in a large airtight plastic bag. Pour the milk into a medium bowl.

Heat the deep fryer to 340°F according to the manufacturer's instructions. To assemble, dip each onion into the flour, then the milk and back into the flour. Shake off any excess flour. Place 1 onion in the deep fryer and cook for 5 minutes. Turn the onion as needed to brown evenly. Repeat with the remaining onion. Make the dip by blending the sour cream, chili powder and 1 teaspoon of Cajun seasoning. Serve with the onion blossoms. Serves 8.

Smoked Salmon & Cream Cheese Wontons

12 oz. cream cheese, softened

6 oz. smoked salmon, flaked in small pieces

2 T. onion, minced

1 clove garlic, minced

12 wonton wrappers

oil for frying

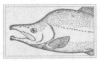 Prepare the salmon filling by combining the cream cheese, salmon, onion and garlic. Place 1 rounded tablespoon of filling on each wonton wrapper. Moisten the edges of the wonton with water and seal into triangles. Heat the deep fryer to 375°F according to the manufacturer's instructions. Place 3-4 wonton in the fryer and cook for 3-4 minutes, or until golden and crispy. Repeat with the remaining wonton. Serves 6.

Restaurant-Style Potato Strips

3 large baking potatoes   salt to taste
oil for frying

 Peel the potatoes. Using an automatic or hand-held vegetable peeler, peel thin, long strips of each potato. Place the potato strips in a large bowl and cover completely with cold water. Let stand for 1 hour. Remove the potatoes from the water, drain and pat completely dry with paper towels.

Heat the deep fryer to 375°F according to the manufacturer's instructions. Carefully place 4 to 6 potato strips in the fryer and fry for 2 minutes or until very crisp. Remove and drain on absorbent paper. Repeat with the remaining potato strips. Salt the potato strips to taste and serve while warm. Keep any leftover potato strips in an airtight plastic bag. Serves 3-6.

Twice-Fried & Super-Crispy French Fries

4 baking potatoes, skins removed   salt to taste
oil for frying

Cut the potatoes into matchstick thin pieces. Place in a large bowl of water and allow them to sit for 1 hour. Drain and dry completely. Heat the deep fryer to 340°F according to the manufacturer's instructions. Place a handful of French fries in the deep fryer and cook for 2-3 minutes. Remove and drain on absorbent paper. Repeat with the remaining fries. When all of the fries have cooled to room temperature, reheat the fryer to 375°F. Deep fry the potatoes as before, cooking for an additional 1-2 minutes, or until very crispy. Repeat with the remaining potatoes and serve immediately. Serves 4.

Deep-Fried Zucchini Appetizers

4 fresh zucchini	1/4 t. black pepper
1 egg, beaten	1/4 t. garlic powder
1 c. seasoned bread crumbs	oil for frying

 Wash and dry the zucchini. Cut into slices ½-inch thick. Heat the deep fryer to 375°F according to the manufacturer's instructions. Combine in a shallow dish the bread crumbs, pepper and garlic powder. Dip 1 slice of zucchini into the egg and then into the bread crumb mixture. Place 5-6 breaded zucchini slices in the fryer and fry for 2-3 minutes, or until golden and crispy. Drain on absorbent paper. Repeat with the remaining slices. Serves 8.

Soy-Sesame Chicken Bites

1 T. soy sauce
1/2 c. sesame seeds
1 c. seasoned bread crumbs

1 lb. roasted chicken breast, cut into 1/2-inch cubes
3 eggs, beaten
oil for frying

 Mix together the soy sauce, sesame seeds and bread crumbs in a shallow bowl. Heat the deep fryer to 375°F according to the manufacturer's instructions. Place each piece of chicken in the eggs and then roll in the bread crumb mixture. Fry 4-5 cubes of chicken for 2 minutes, turning once. Drain on absorbent paper and repeat with the remaining chicken. Makes about 30 pieces.

Classic Monte Cristo Sandwiches

12 slices firm white bread, crusts removed

4 oz. Gruyère cheese, cut into 8 thin slices

8 oz. cooked ham, cut into 8 slices

2 T. prepared spicy mustard

8 oz. cooked chicken breast, cut into 8 slices

4 eggs, beaten

1 c. milk

oil for frying

Assemble the sandwiches by placing 4 slices of cheese on 4 pieces of the bread. Top the cheese with the ham slices. Spread each ham slice with spicy mustard and top with another piece of bread. Cover with another slice of cheese. Top with the sliced chicken and another dollop of spicy mustard. Layer the last piece of bread over each of the 4 sandwiches. Cut each sandwich into fourths and secure the quarters with toothpicks.

Heat the deep fryer to 375°F according to the manufacturer's instructions. Beat the eggs and milk together and quickly dip each sandwich into the mixture. Fry 4 sandwich quarters at a time for 2 minutes. Turn and fry for 2 minutes or until golden brown. Drain on absorbent paper and repeat with the remaining sandwiches. Serves 4.

Twice-Fried Chinese Chicken Wings

Soy Ginger Marinade
1/2 c. soy sauce
2 T. rice wine vinegar
2 cloves garlic, minced
1 t. sugar
2 green onions, thinly sliced

10 chicken wings
1 egg white, beaten to stiff peaks
1/2 c. cornstarch
1 t. baking powder
1 t. five-spice powder
oil for frying

 Combine the marinade ingredients in a plastic bag. Remove the chicken wing tips and discard. Cut the chicken at the joint to create 2 pieces from each wing. Place the chicken in the marinade and refrigerate for 4 hours or overnight. Remove the chicken from the marinade and discard the marinade.

Heat the deep fryer to 355°F according to the manufacturer's instructions. Dip 1 chicken wing in the egg white. Combine the cornstarch with the baking powder and five-spice powder. Roll the chicken wing in the cornstarch mixture. Repeat with 2 additional pieces of chicken. Fry 3-4 pieces of chicken for 4 minutes, turning once to brown evenly. Remove 1 piece to test for doneness. The chicken should be cooked completely through. If not, continue frying for 1-2 minutes. Drain the chicken wings on absorbent paper and repeat with the remaining chicken.

Fried Lasagna Bruschetta

8 lasagna noodles, cooked and drained

2 medium tomatoes, chopped

2 cloves garlic, minced

2 T. fresh parsley minced

1/2 t. salt

1/2 t. black pepper

1 T. extra virgin olive oil

oil for frying

 Heat the deep fryer to 375°F according to the manufacturer's instructions. Cut each noodle into 3 equal pieces and pat dry. Fry 3-4 pieces of the lasagna noodles for 2-3 minutes and drain on absorbent paper. Repeat with the remaining noodles.

Prepare the bruschetta topping by combining in a medium bowl the chopped tomatoes, garlic, parsley, salt, pepper and olive oil. Mix well. Place 1 tablespoon of the topping on each square of lasagna and serve immediately. Makes 24 appetizers.

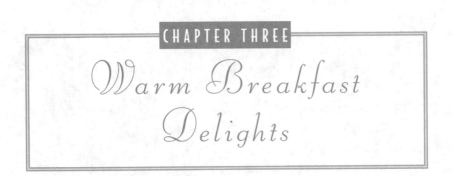

CHAPTER THREE

Warm Breakfast Delights

Ahhh! Nothing says "breakfast" like a warm, fresh, glazed donut first thing in the morning! A glass of just-squeezed orange juice or a hot cup of coffee is the only complement you need to such a delightful start of the day. Inside this chapter you'll find many wonderful deep-fried breakfast treats including cake donuts, raised donuts, bars and fancy treats.

Your deep fryer is the ultimate "breakfast machine." Deep-fried breakfast breads and pastries are fried quickly at high temperatures, resulting in a light texture and less grease absorption inside the food. And, with a wide variety of frostings and toppings included in these recipes, you can customize all of these recipes to suit your favorite tastes!

Maryann's Favorite Honey Spice Donuts

1/2 c. granulated white sugar
2 t. baking powder
1/2 t. baking soda
1 1/2 t. salt
1/2 t. ground nutmeg
3-3 1/2 c. flour (enough for a soft dough)

1/4 c. vegetable oil
1/2 c. honey
1 c. milk
2 t. vanilla
3 eggs
oil for frying

 Using a medium bowl, combine the sugar, baking powder, baking soda, salt, nutmeg and flour. In a large bowl, combine the oil, honey, milk and vanilla. Add the eggs and blend.

Add the dry ingredients slowly, stirring until all of the flour mixture has been added. Add more flour if necessary. The dough will be sticky. Sift a heavy coat of flour onto a clean surface. Turn out the dough and sift another heavy layer of flour over the dough. Using your hands, pat the dough until it is ½-inch thick. Using a donut cutter or 2 glasses (using 1 cup approximately 2-inches in diameter and 1 cup approximately ½-inch in diameter), cut out the donuts as close together as possible, dipping the cutter in the flour between each cut. Transfer the donuts to a floured pan and let rest for 10 minutes.

Heat your Ultrex® Deep Fryer to 375°F according to the instructions. Place 2-3 donuts in the fryer and cook for 2 minutes. Turn and cook for an additional 2 minutes, or until completely golden brown. Using a slotted spoon, transfer the donuts to a pan lined with paper towels. Repeat with the remaining donuts. When the donuts are cool, sift powdered or granulated sugar and cinnamon over the top of the donuts. You may also use nutmeg sugar made from ½ t. ground nutmeg mixed with 1 cup of sugar. These donuts can be frozen ahead and reheated in a warm oven just before serving. Makes about 20 donuts.

Homemade Cinnamon Twists

2 c. prepared baking mix
3 T. sugar
1/2 t. ground cinnamon
1/2 t. ground nutmeg
1/4 c. milk
1 egg, beaten
oil for frying

Cinnamon Topping:
1 c. sugar
1 t. ground cinnamon

 In a large bowl, combine the baking mix, sugar, cinnamon, nutmeg, milk and egg. Blend well for 1 minute. Turn the dough onto a lightly floured board and roll to a thickness of ⅓-inch. Cut with a lightly floured donut cutter. Remove the donut holes and reserve. Twist each donut to make a figure "8" and set aside. In a small bowl, combine the sugar and ground cinnamon and set aside.

Heat the deep fryer to 355°F according to the manufacturer's instructions. Place 2 to 3 twists into the fryer and fry for about 2 minutes. Turn and fry for 2 minutes, or until golden brown on both sides and cooked through. Remove from the fryer and drain on absorbent paper. Repeat with the remaining twists.

While the twists are still warm, dust each with the cinnamon/sugar mixture and serve immediately. If desired, you may also deep fry the donut holes for 2 minutes each and roll in the cinnamon/sugar to serve. Makes 10-12 twists.

Raised & Glazed Donuts

1 1/2 c. milk

1 c. sugar

3/4 c. butter or margarine, softened

1 t. ground cinnamon

1 t. salt

3 1/4 oz. pkgs. active dry yeast

1/2 c. water, 105-115°F

4 eggs, beaten

7 1/2 c. flour

oil for frying

Donut Glaze:

1/2 c. boiling water

1 c. powdered sugar

 In a large bowl, combine the milk, sugar, butter, cinnamon and salt. In a small bowl, combine the yeast and warm water and stir to dissolve. Add the yeast and water to the large bowl. Add the eggs and 3 cups of the flour. Mix well to combine. Add enough remaining flour to make a soft dough. Turn the dough onto a lightly floured board and knead for 5 to 10 minutes or until smooth and elastic. Place in a bowl sprayed with cooking spray and turn. Cover with a clean cloth and let rise in a warm place until doubled in size. This will take about 1½ hours.

Punch down the dough. On a lightly floured surface, pat out one half of the dough until the dough is uniformly ½-inch thick. Use a lightly floured donut cutter to cut the donuts and place on a lightly floured board. Pat out the remaining dough and cut the donuts as above. Cover the donuts and let rise again. This will take approximately 30-45 minutes. Reserve the donut holes to fry after the donuts or discard.

Heat the deep fryer to 375°F according to the manufacturer's instructions. Place 2 to 3 donuts in the fryer and cook for 2 minutes. Turn and cook for 1 minute, or until golden brown and crispy. Remove and drain on absorbent paper. Repeat this process with the remaining donuts. Fry the donut holes for 1-2 minutes, if desired. While the donuts are cooling, mix together the water and powdered sugar and blend completely. Dip the warm donuts in the glaze and set aside. Donuts may be eaten warm or cold. To store the donuts, carefully pack in aluminum foil or plastic bags and refrigerate. You may reheat donuts by micro-waving them for 5-6 seconds on HIGH. Makes about 24 donuts.

Tender Cake Donuts

4 1/4 c. flour
3 1/2 t. baking powder
1 t. salt
1/2 t. ground cinnamon
1/4 t. ground nutmeg
3 eggs, beaten

1 t. vanilla flavoring
3/4 c. sugar
1/4 c. butter or margarine,
  softened
3/4 c. milk
oil for frying

 In a large bowl, combine the flour, baking powder, salt, cinnamon and nutmeg. Blend well. Add the eggs, vanilla, sugar, butter and milk and blend again until thoroughly combined. Turn the dough onto a lightly floured board and pat or roll into a uniform ½-inch thickness. Cut the donuts using a lightly floured donut cutter.

Heat the deep fryer to 375°F according to the manufacturer's instructions. Place 2 to 3 donuts in the fryer and fry for about 2 minutes. Turn the donuts and fry for about 1 minute, or until both sides are crispy and golden brown. Remove the donuts and drain on absorbent paper. Repeat with the remaining donuts. Serve plain or dusted with powdered sugar. Makes about 16 donuts.

Deep-Fried French Toast

2 eggs
1/3 c. milk
1/4 t. salt

8 slices bread, cut in 1-inch thick slices
oil for frying

 In a wide dish, mix the eggs with the milk and salt. Heat the deep fryer to 375°F according to the manufacturer's instructions. Place 1 slice of bread in the egg and milk mixture and allow the excess to drip back into the dish. Fry the slice of bread for 2 minutes, turning once. Drain on absorbent paper and repeat with the remaining slices. Serve while warm. Serves 4.

Banana Donuts with Walnut Crumb Topping

1 c. milk	**Walnut Crumb Topping:**
1 c. sugar	1/2 c. walnuts, finely chopped
2 eggs, beaten	1/4 c. sugar
1/2 c. very ripe bananas, pureed	1 T. flour
1/2 c. butter or margarine, softened	2 T. butter, softened
1 t. ground cinnamon	
1 t. salt	
4 1/2 c. flour	
2 t. baking powder	
oil for frying	

 In a large bowl, combine the milk, sugar, eggs, bananas, butter, cinnamon and salt. Add 3 cups of the flour. Mix well to combine. Add enough remaining flour to make a soft dough. Turn the dough onto a lightly floured board and knead lightly for 30 seconds. Pat out to ⅓-inch thick. Cut with a floured donut cutter.

Heat the deep fryer to 375°F according to the manufacturer's instructions. Place 2 to 3 donuts in the fryer and cook for 2 minutes. Turn and cook for 1 minute, or until golden brown and crispy. Remove and drain on absorbent paper. Repeat this process with the remaining donuts. Fry the donut holes for 1-2 minutes, if desired. Toss together with a fork the walnuts, sugar and flour. Cut in the butter until the mixture is uniformly small crumbs. Gently press the warm donuts in the walnut crumb topping and set aside. Donuts may be eaten warm or cold. To store the donuts, carefully pack in aluminum foil or plastic bags and refrigerate. You may reheat the donuts by microwaving them for 5-6 seconds on HIGH. Makes about 16 donuts.

Harvest Pumpkin Bars with Maple Frosting

3/4 c. milk

1 c. sugar

2 T. butter or margarine, softened

1/2 t. ground cinnamon

1/2 t. ground nutmeg

1/2 c. prepared pumpkin puree

1/2 t. salt

2 eggs, beaten

3 t. baking powder

3 1/3 c. flour

oil for frying

Maple Frosting:

2 c. powdered sugar

1/4 c. hot water

3 t. butter or margarine, melted

1/4 t. maple flavoring

 In a large bowl, combine with an electric mixer the milk, sugar, butter, cinnamon, nutmeg, pumpkin and salt. Add the eggs. Blend again. Combine the baking powder and the flour and gradually add to the dough. Mix to make a soft dough. Turn the dough onto a lightly floured board and knead lightly for 1 minute. Roll the dough to a rectangle about 3 inches in length and 16 inches in width. Cut into bars 1-inch wide.

Heat the deep fryer to 375°F according to the manufacturer's instructions. Place 3-4 bars in the fryer and cook for 2 minutes. Turn and cook for 1 minute, or until golden brown and crispy. Remove and drain on absorbent paper. Repeat this process with the remaining bars. In a small bowl, combine the powdered sugar, water, butter and maple flavoring. Using a wide spatula or knife, frost each bar with the maple frosting. To store the bars, carefully pack in aluminum foil or plastic bags and refrigerate. You may reheat the bars by microwaving them for 5-6 seconds on HIGH. Makes about 16 bars.

Mini Breakfast Churros

1 1/2 c. milk

1 c. sugar

3/4 c. butter or margarine, softened

1 t. ground cinnamon

1 t. salt

3 1/4 oz. pkgs. active dry yeast

1/2 c. water, 105-115°F

4 eggs, beaten

7 1/2 c. flour

oil for frying

Sugar Topping:

1 c. sugar

1 t. ground cinnamon

 In a large bowl, combine the milk, sugar, butter, cinnamon and salt. In a small bowl, combine the yeast and warm water and stir to dissolve. Add the yeast and water to the large bowl. Add the eggs and 3 cups of the flour. Mix well to combine. Add enough remaining flour to make a soft dough. Turn the dough onto a lightly floured board and knead for 5 to 10 minutes or until smooth and elastic. Place in a bowl sprayed with cooking spray and turn. Cover with a clean cloth and let rise in a warm place until doubled in size 1½ to 2 hours.

Punch down the dough. Fill a pastry bag with a large star tip. Press the dough into bars about 3 inches in length onto a lightly floured board. Cover and let rise again. This will take approximately 30-45 minutes.

Heat the deep fryer to 375°F according to the manufacturer's instructions. Place 3-4 churros in the fryer and cook for 1 minute. Turn and cook for 1 minute, or until golden brown and crispy. Remove and drain on absorbent paper. Repeat this process with the remaining churros. While the churros are cooling, mix together the sugar and cinnamon in a small bowl. Sprinkle the sugar/cinnamon over each churro. Churros may be eaten warm or cold. To store the churros, carefully pack in aluminum foil or plastic bags and refrigerate. Makes about 36 churros.

Fresh Strawberry & Cream Cheese Bars

3/4 c. milk

1 c. sugar

1/2 c. butter or margarine, softened

1/2 t. ground cinnamon

1/2 c. pureed fresh or frozen strawberries

1/2 t. salt

1/4 t. red food coloring (if desired)

2 eggs, beaten

3 1/2 c. flour

oil for frying

Cream Cheese Frosting:

1 c. powdered sugar

1/2 c. cream cheese, softened

3 T. milk

1/4 t. vanilla flavoring

 In a large bowl, combine with an electric mixer the milk, sugar, butter, cinnamon, strawberries and salt. Add the food coloring if desired. Add the eggs and 3 cups of the flour. Mix well to combine. Add enough remaining flour to make a soft dough. Turn the dough onto a lightly floured board and pat into a rectangle about 3 inches in length and 16 inches in width. Cut into bars 1-inch in width using a sharp knife.

Heat the deep fryer to 375°F according to the manufacturer's instructions. Place 1-2 bars in the fryer and cook for 2 minutes. Turn and cook for 1 minute, or until golden brown and crispy. Remove and drain on absorbent paper. Repeat this process with the remaining bars. Using an electric mixer, combine the powdered sugar, cream cheese, milk and vanilla flavoring. Blend well at a high speed for 2 minutes. Using a wide spatula or knife, frost each bar with the cream cheese frosting. To store the bars, carefully pack in aluminum foil or plastic bags and refrigerate. Makes about 16 bars.

Double Chocolate Donuts

3 1/2 c. flour

2 T. baking powder

1 t. salt

1/2 t. ground nutmeg

1/2 t. ground cinnamon

1/2 c. cocoa

1 1/2 c. sugar

1/4 c. butter or margarine, melted

1 c. mashed potatoes

2 eggs, beaten

1/2 c. milk

oil for frying

Chocolate Frosting:

2 c. powdered sugar

4 T. hot water

1 oz. unsweetened chocolate, melted

1 T. butter or margarine

 In a large bowl, mix together the flour, baking powder, salt, nutmeg, cinnamon, cocoa and sugar. Add the butter, mashed potatoes, eggs and milk. Blend completely. Turn the dough onto a lightly floured board and pat or roll into a uniform ½-inch thickness. Cut the donuts using a lightly floured donut cutter.

Heat the deep fryer to 375°F according to the manufacturer's instructions. Place 2 to 3 donuts in the fryer and fry for about 2 minutes. Turn the donuts and fry for about 1 minute, or until both sides are crispy and golden brown. Remove the donuts and drain on absorbent paper. Repeat with the remaining donuts. To make the frosting, use an electric mixer to blend the powdered sugar, water, chocolate and butter. Whip until smooth and glossy. Dip each donut into the frosting and allow to cool. Makes about 16 donuts.

Rich Glazed Buttermilk Bars

1 c. buttermilk	1 t. baking soda
1 c. sugar	3 1/2 c. flour
2 T. butter or margarine, softened	oil for frying
1/2 t. ground cinnamon	
1 t. vanilla flavoring	2 c. powdered sugar
1/2 t. salt	1/3 c. milk
2 eggs, beaten	1/4 t. vanilla flavoring
2 t. baking powder	

 In a large bowl, combine with an electric mixer the buttermilk, sugar, butter, cinnamon, vanilla and salt. Beat in the eggs to blend. Add the baking powder, baking soda and 3 cups of the flour. Mix well to combine. Add enough remaining flour to make a soft dough. On a lightly floured surface, pat out a rectangle 5 inches by 10 inches and ½-inch thick. Using a sharp knife, measure and cut the dough to make 2-inch by 5-inch bars. Cut the bars horizontally again to make 2-inch by 2½-inch bars. Pat out the remaining half of the dough and cut into bars as above.

Heat the deep fryer to 375°F according to the manufacturer's instructions. Place 2-3 bars in the fryer and cook for 3 minutes. Turn and cook for 2 minutes, or until golden brown and crispy. Remove and drain on absorbent paper. Repeat this process with the remaining bars. Using a whisk or electric mixer, blend the powdered sugar, milk and vanilla. Blend well for 2 minutes. Dip each bar into the glaze and allow them to set for 30 minutes. To store the bars, carefully pack in aluminum foil or plastic bags and refrigerate. Makes about 20 bars.

Raspberry Jelly-Filled Donuts

3/4 c. milk
1/4 c. sugar
1/4 c. butter or margarine, softened
1 t. salt
1 1/4 oz. pkg. active dry yeast
1/4 c. water, 105-115°F
1 egg
3 1/2 - 4 c. flour
oil for frying

Donut Filling:
1 c. raspberry jelly, whisked until smooth

Donut Glaze:
1 c. powdered sugar
1/4 c. milk

 In a large bowl, combine the milk, sugar, butter and salt. In a small bowl, combine the yeast and warm water and stir to dissolve. Add the yeast and water to the large bowl. Add the egg and 3 cups of the flour. Mix well to combine. Add enough remaining flour to make a soft dough. Turn the dough onto a lightly floured board and knead for 5 to 10 minutes or until smooth and elastic. Place in a bowl sprayed with cooking spray and turn. Cover with a clean cloth and let rise in a warm place until doubled in size, 1½-2 hours.

Punch down the dough. On a lightly floured surface, pat out the dough until the dough is uniformly ½-inch thick. Use a lightly floured cookie cutter (the cookie cutter should not cut a hole in the center of the donuts), cut the donuts and place on a lightly floured board. Cover the donuts and let rise again, 30-45 minutes.

Heat the deep fryer to 375°F according to the manufacturer's instructions. Place 2 to 3 donuts in the fryer and cook for 2 minutes. Turn and cook for 1 minute, or until golden brown and crispy. Remove and drain on absorbent paper. Repeat this process with the remaining donuts. Using a pastry bag and a coupler with a small filler tip, squeeze 1 tablespoon of jelly into one side of each donut. While the donuts are cooling, mix together the powdered sugar and milk and blend completely. Dip the warm donuts in the glaze and set aside. The donuts may be eaten warm or cold. To store the donuts, carefully pack in aluminum foil or plastic bags and refrigerate. You may reheat the donuts by microwaving them for 5-6 seconds on HIGH. Makes about 20 donuts.

Bavarian Lemon Crème-Filled Fancies

1 1/2 c. milk	7-8 c. flour
1/2 c. butter or margarine, softened	oil for frying
1 c. sugar	1 c. powdered sugar
4 eggs, beaten	
1 t. vanilla flavoring	**Bavarian Crème**
3 pkgs. 1/4 oz. active dry yeast	3 oz. pkg. lemon flavored gelatin
1/2 c. water, 105-115°F	2 c. boiling water
1 1/2 t. salt	1 c. heavy cream, whipped

 In a large bowl, combine with an electric mixer the milk, butter, sugar, eggs and vanilla. In a small bowl, combine the yeast and warm water and stir to dissolve. Add the yeast and water to the large bowl. Add the salt and 6 cups of the flour. Mix well to combine. Add enough remaining flour to make a soft dough. Turn the dough onto a lightly floured board and knead for 5 to 10 minutes or until smooth and elastic. Place in a bowl sprayed with cooking spray and turn. Cover with a clean cloth and let rise in a warm place until doubled in size, about 1½-2 hours.

Punch down the dough. On a lightly floured surface, pat out one half of dough into a rectangle 5 inches by 10 inches and ½-inch thick. Using a sharp knife, measure and cut the dough to make 2-inch by 5-inch bars. Cut the dough again horizontally to make bars 2-inches by 2½-inches. Pat out the remaining half of the dough and cut into bars as above. Place on a lightly floured board and cover to rise again, approximately 30-45 minutes.

Heat the deep fryer to 375°F according to manufacturer's instructions. Place 2-3 bars in the fryer and cook for 2 minutes. Turn and cook for 1 minute, or until golden brown and crispy. Remove and drain on absorbent paper. Repeat this process with the remaining bars. To make the *Bavarian Crème*, prepare the gelatin and water as directed on the package. When the gelatin is cooled to a thick, but not set consistency, fold in the whipped cream. Using a pastry bag with a coupler and medium filler tip, pipe the crème into the side of each bar in two places, filling each place with about 1 tablespoon of crème. Dust each bar with powdered sugar. Serve immediately or store the bars, carefully packed in aluminum foil or plastic bags and refrigerated. Makes about 20 bars.

Bakery-Style Cinnamon Krispies

1 pkg. 1/4 oz. active dry yeast	**Cinnamon Streusel:**
1 1/4 c. milk, 110-115°F	1/2 c. sugar
1/4 c. butter	1/2 c. brown sugar, packed
1/4 c. sugar	1/2 t. ground cinnamon
1 t. salt	1/4 t. ground nutmeg
1 egg, beaten	
3 1/2-4 c. flour	**Krispie Glaze:**
oil for frying	2 c. powdered sugar
1/4 c. butter, melted	1/3 c. milk
	1 t. vanilla flavoring
	2 T. butter, melted

 In a small bowl, sprinkle the yeast over the milk and stir well to dissolve. Set aside. In a large bowl with an electric mixer, combine the butter, sugar, salt and the egg and beat until well-blended. Add the yeast mixture and approximately 3 cups of flour and blend again. Continue adding flour until the dough is soft and no longer tacky to the touch. Turn out onto a lightly floured board and knead for 5-10 minutes or until smooth and elastic. Lightly coat a large bowl with cooking spray and place the dough in the bowl. Turn the dough and cover the bowl with a clean cloth. Put the dough in a warm place to rise until doubled, about 1½ hours.

Punch down the dough and roll into a rectangle about 9-inches by 18-inches in size. Brush the dough with the melted butter. In a small bowl, combine the streusel ingredients and sprinkle over the dough evenly. Roll the rectangle in jelly roll fashion and cut into slices 1-inch thick. Cover with waxed paper and press each slice into a flat circle about ¼-inch in thickness. Place the krispies on a lightly floured board, cover and let rise again, about 30-45 minutes.

Heat the deep fryer to 375°F. Fry 1 or 2 krispies at a time for 2 minutes. Turn and fry for an additional 2 minutes. Remove the krispies and drain on absorbent paper. Repeat the frying process for the remaining krispies. In a small bowl, make the glaze by mixing thoroughly the powdered sugar, milk, vanilla and butter. Drizzle the glaze over each krispie and cool. Makes about 18 krispies.

Tropical Pineapple Donuts with Coconut Frosting

1/2 c. light cream

1/4 c. frozen pineapple juice concentrate, thawed

2 eggs, beaten

3–3 1/2 c. flour

1 c. sugar

3 t. baking powder

1/2 t. salt

1/2 t. cinnamon

oil for frying

Coconut Frosting:

2 c. powdered sugar

1/4 c. warm water

1 T. butter, melted

1/2 t. coconut flavoring

1/2 c. coconut, shredded

In a large bowl, combine the cream, pineapple juice and eggs. Beat well until completely blended. Add the flour, sugar, baking powder, salt and cinnamon. Beat again until the dough leaves the sides of the bowl and the ingredients are incorporated very well. Add additional flour if the dough seems too soft. On a lightly floured board, roll or pat the dough to a uniform ½-inch thickness. Cut the donuts with a floured donut cutter. Save the doughnut holes to fry after the donuts.

Heat the deep fryer to 375°F according to the manufacturer's instructions. Place 2-3 donuts in the fryer and cook for 2 minutes. Turn and cook for an additional 1 minute, or until the donuts are cooked through and golden brown. Place on absorbent paper and repeat the process with the remaining donuts. Make the frosting by combining the sugar, water, butter and coconut flavoring. Whisk or beat with the electric mixer to thoroughly blend. Dip each warm donut into the coconut frosting and then dip each donut into the shredded coconut. Allow the donuts to dry for 30 minutes and serve. If desired, you may store these donuts by wrapping them in aluminum foil or placing them in an airtight plastic container. Refrigerate to keep them fresh for as long as possible. Makes 16 donuts.

Old-Fashioned Blueberry Donuts

4 1/2 c. flour	3/4 c. sugar
3 1/2 t. baking powder	1/4 c. butter or margarine, softened
1 t. salt	
1/2 t. ground cinnamon	3/4 c. milk
1/4 t. ground nutmeg	1 c. fresh or canned blueberries, rinsed and drained
1/8 t. ground cloves	
3 eggs, beaten	oil for frying
1 t. vanilla flavoring	

 In a large bowl, combine the flour, baking powder, salt, cinnamon, nutmeg and cloves. Blend well. Add the eggs, vanilla, sugar, butter and milk and blend again until thoroughly combined. Fold in the blueberries. Turn the dough onto a lightly floured board and pat or roll into a uniform ½-inch thickness. Cut the donuts using a lightly floured donut cutter.

Heat the deep fryer to 375°F according to the manufacturer's instructions. Place 2 to 3 donuts in the fryer and fry for about 2 minutes. Turn the donuts and fry for about 1 minute, or until both sides are crispy and golden brown. Remove the donuts and drain on absorbent paper. Repeat with the remaining donuts. Serve plain or dusted with powdered sugar. Makes about 18 donuts.

Applesauce & Spice Donuts

4 1/2 c. flour	3 eggs, beaten
3 1/2 t. baking powder	1 t. vanilla flavoring
1 t. salt	3/4 c. sugar
1/2 t. ground cinnamon	1/4 c. butter or margarine,
1/4 t. ground nutmeg	softened
1/8 t. ground cloves	1/2 c. milk
3/4 c. prepared applesauce	oil for frying

 In a large bowl, combine the flour, baking powder, salt, cinnamon, nutmeg and cloves. Blend well. Add the applesauce, eggs, vanilla, sugar, butter and milk and blend again until thoroughly combined. Turn the dough onto a lightly floured board and pat or roll into a uniform ½-inch thickness. Cut the donuts using a lightly floured donut cutter.

Heat the deep fryer to 375°F according to the manufacturer's instructions. Place 2 to 3 donuts in the fryer and fry for about 2 minutes. Turn the donuts and fry for about 1 minute, or until both sides are crispy and golden brown. Remove the donuts and drain on absorbent paper. Repeat with the remaining donuts. Serve plain or dusted with powdered sugar. Makes about 20 donuts.

New Orleans Beignets

1 pkg. prepared Hot Roll mix	powdered sugar
1/2 c. sugar	oil for frying

 Prepare the rolls according to the package instructions. When the dough is ready to be shaped, divide the dough in half. On a board that has been lightly dusted with 1/2 cup of sugar, roll one-half of the dough into a 9" x 12" rectangle. Cut the rectangle into 12 squares. Repeat with the remaining dough and allow the squares to rise again for 30-45 minutes. Heat the deep fryer to 375°F according to the manufacturer's instructions. Fry 2-3 beignets at a time for 2 minutes. Turn and fry for 2-3 minutes, or until golden brown and cooked through. Drain on absorbent paper and repeat with the remaining beignets. Dust each beignet with powdered sugar before serving. Makes 24.

CHAPTER FOUR

Homestyle Entrée Favorites

The process of deep-frying meats, poultry and seafood has been used globally by cooks for several decades. The quick-cooking method of frying at high heat allows foods to retain tenderness and the light crispiness of the batters and breading in oil is the perfect accompaniment to most cuts of meat, poultry and seafood.

In this chapter you will find some delightful recipes that will take you back in time—*Beer-Battered Fish & Chips*, *Grandma's Deep-Fried Chicken* and *Crispy Pork Chops in Savory Herb Gravy*. You'll also find some surprisingly delicious creations that will bring everyone to the table in record time— *Gourmet Lemon Chicken*, *Golden Veal Cutlets with Tomato & Basil Marinara Sauce* and *Bayou Fried Catfish*.

As you sample the recipes in this chapter, you will also want to create your own family favorites. The only specific rules for deep frying are to maintain the proper temperatures in the deep fryer and to cook meats, poultry and seafood as dictated by food safety guidelines. Other than that, feel free to experiment. Mix and match batters and breadings found here with the meats, poultry and seafood your family likes best. Try a variety of herbs and spices in your deep-frying batters and breading to lend an exotic touch to your meal. Enjoy all the goodness that deep frying brings to your family!

French Fried Nantucket Clams

1 pt. fresh clams	2 eggs
1/2 c. flour	2 c. dry saltine crackers, finely ground
1 t. salt	
1/2 t. black pepper, freshly ground	oil for frying

 Shuck the clams and clean thoroughly. In a medium bowl, combine the flour, salt and pepper. In a separate bowl, beat the eggs and set aside. Place the cracker crumbs on a large dinner plate.

Heat the deep fryer to 355°F according to the manufacturer's instructions. Prepare the clams for frying by coating each with the flour and spices, dipping each in the eggs and coating with the cracker crumbs. Fry 3 to 4 clams at a time for 2-3 minutes, turning once during frying. Drain the fried clams on absorbent paper and repeat the process with the remaining clams. Serves 4.

Herbed Beef & Potato Croquettes

1 lb. lean ground beef	4 c. mashed potatoes
1 t. salt	2 eggs, beaten
1/2 t. black pepper	2 c. seasoned bread crumbs
1 medium onion, chopped	oil for frying
2 T. fresh parsley, minced	

 Over medium heat, brown the ground beef and drain any excess fat from the pan. Add the salt and pepper, onion and parsley. Place a large scoop (about the size of a lemon) of mashed potatoes on a lightly floured surface. Put a heaping tablespoon of meat filling in the middle of the potatoes and completely seal the potatoes over the meat. Form an oval egg-shape with the potatoes. Dip each potato oval in the beaten eggs and roll in the seasoned bread crumbs.

Heat the deep fryer to 340°F. Deep fry 3-4 croquettes at a time for 2 minutes on one side. Turn the croquettes and fry for 2-3 minutes or until cooked through and golden brown. Drain on absorbent paper and repeat with the remaining croquettes. Serves 4.

Crispy Pork Chops in Savory Herb Gravy

2 eggs, beaten	1/2 t. black pepper
1/2 c. Parmesan cheese	2 T. fresh parsley, finely minced
2 c. saltine crackers, finely ground	1 T. fresh sage, finely minced
1 t. black pepper	1 T. fresh thyme, finely minced
4 lean pork loin chops	3 T. flour
2 c. beef broth	1/2 c. water
1 T. browning sauce	oil for frying
1 t. salt	

 Place the eggs in a wide, shallow bowl. Combine in a medium bowl the Parmesan cheese, saltine crackers and black pepper. Heat the deep fryer to 375°F according to the manufacturer's instructions. Dip each chop in the egg and then in the cheese crackers, turning to coat both sides. Fry 1-2 chops at a time for 5-6 minutes. Turn and fry for 1-2 minutes, or until cooked through and golden brown. Drain on absorbent paper. To prepare the gravy, heat the broth, browning sauce, salt, black pepper, parsley, sage and thyme to a boil. Mix the flour with the water in a small bowl and add to the boiling water. Stir the gravy to incorporate the flour and lower the heat to simmer. Simmer for 5 minutes, stirring constantly. To serve, pour the gravy over the individual pork chops. Makes 4 servings.

Sweet & Sour Chicken & Vegetables

1 1/2 c. milk	2 T. soy sauce
1/2 c. vegetable oil	1 green pepper, roughly chopped
2 T. baking powder	2 carrots, cut into 1/4-inch thick slices
1 t. salt	
2 c. flour	1 red pepper, roughly chopped
2 lbs. uncooked, skinless chicken breast, cut into 1-inch squares	1 small white onion, peeled and roughly chopped
	1 c. canned pineapple chunks
1/4 c. cornstarch	oil for frying
1 1/2 c. water	

 In a large bowl, combine the milk, oil, baking powder, salt and flour. Blend until completely smooth with a whisk or electric mixer. Heat the deep fryer to 375°F according to the manufacturer's instructions. Dip the chicken pieces in the batter and deep fry 3-5 pieces at a time. Fry for 5-6 minutes, or completely cooked through. Repeat with the remaining chicken. Drain on absorbent paper and place on a large warmed serving platter.

In a large sauté pan, combine the cornstarch and water. Heat and stir until thickened. Add the soy sauce, green pepper, carrots, red pepper, onion and pineapple and cook over low heat for 8-10 minutes. To serve, pour the vegetables and sauce over the chicken and serve immediately. Serves 6.

Chianti Beef in Parmesan & Tomato Risotto

Parmesan & Tomato Risotto:

1 medium onion, finely chopped

2 cloves garlic, minced

1 T. extra virgin olive oil

1 1/2 c. Arborio rice

1/2 c. dried tomatoes, minced

1/2 c. dry white wine

5 c. beef broth, warmed

1/4 c. Parmesan cheese

3/4 c. Chianti or other full-bodied red wine

1 t. black pepper

1 clove garlic, chopped

2 lbs. lean beef, cut into 1/2-inch strips

2 eggs, beaten

1 c. Italian-seasoned breadcrumbs

oil for frying

Sauté the onion and garlic with the olive oil in a large pan until the vegetables are translucent. Add the rice, wine and tomatoes and mix well. Sauté over medium heat until the wine has been absorbed. Add the beef broth 1 cup at a time until the broth is absorbed each time. Cook over very low heat for 5 minutes. Add the Parmesan cheese just before serving.

Place the Chianti, pepper, garlic and beef in a shallow glass dish and refrigerate for 1 hour. Discard the marinade. Heat the deep fryer to 355°F according to the manufacturer's instructions. To assemble the beef, dip each piece in the egg, then in the breadcrumbs. Place in the deep fryer, 3-5 pieces at a time and fry for 4-5 minutes, turning once during frying. Drain on absorbent paper. To serve, spoon the risotto onto a large serving platter and top with the beef. Makes 6 servings.

Spicy Asian Chicken

1 lb. boneless chicken breast, cut into strips 1/2-inch x 2-inches

1 t. ground chili powder

1 T. dry sherry

1 T. soy sauce

1 t. sugar

1 T. fresh ginger, finely minced

2 T. green onions, minced

3 cloves garlic, minced

1 c. flour

oil for frying

 Place the chicken in a large plastic bag and add the chili powder, sherry, soy sauce, sugar, ginger, onions and garlic. Marinate for at least 2 hours or overnight. Discard the marinade and heat the deep fryer to 355°F according to the manufacturer's instructions. Dredge the chicken lightly in the flour and deep fry 3-5 pieces at a time, for about 5-6 minutes. Turn and fry for 1-2 minutes or until the chicken is completely cooked through. Repeat the process with the remaining chicken strips. Serve over rice or Chinese noodles. Serves 4.

Southern Fried Crab Cakes

2 c. flour
1 3/4 c. water
3 T. vegetable oil
3 t. baking powder
1/4 t. ground paprika
1/2 t. salt
1 lb. fresh or canned crabmeat, cleaned and shredded

1 c. dry Italian-seasoned breadcrumbs
2 eggs, beaten
1/2 t. salt
1 c. prepared cocktail sauce
oil for frying

In a large bowl, combine the flour, water, oil, baking powder, paprika and salt. Mix together thoroughly. In a medium bowl, mix together the crabmeat, breadcrumbs, eggs and salt. Blend well. Form the crabmeat mixture into 4 balls the size of baseballs and flatten to form cakes.

Heat the deep fryer to 340°F according to the manufacturer's instructions. Coat each crab cake in the batter. Place 2 of the cakes in the deep fryer and cook, turning once, for 5 minutes. Drain on absorbent paper. Remove the cakes to a warm platter and repeat the process with the remaining crab cakes. Serve with the prepared cocktail sauce. Serves 4.

Beer-Battered Fish & Chips

4 baking potatoes, peeled and sliced thinly	1 t. salt
oil for frying	2 t. baking powder
1 c. cold beer	1 t. dried parsley
3/4 c. milk	2 lbs. mild white fish fillets
2 eggs, beaten	1/2 c. prepared tartar sauce
1 1/2 c. flour	oil for frying

 Place the potatoes in a bowl, cover with water and let stand for 1 hour. Drain and dry the potatoes with paper towels. Heat the deep fryer to 375°F according to the manufacturer's instructions. Place a small handful of potatoes in the fryer and cook for 2 minutes. Turn and cook for 1 minute. Drain on absorbent paper and keep warm in the oven while preparing the fish. In a large bowl, combine the beer, milk and eggs. Blend well. Add the flour, salt, baking powder and parsley and blend again until smooth.

Heat the deep fryer to 355°F. Dip each fillet in the batter and place 2-3 fillets in the deep fryer and cook for 5-6 minutes. Turn carefully and fry for 1-2 minutes, or until the fish is cooked through and crispy brown. Drain the fillets on absorbent paper and repeat the frying process with the remaining fillets. Serve warm with the chips and prepared tartar sauce. Serves 4.

Grandma's Deep-Fried Chicken

1 c. flour	2 eggs, beaten
1 t. salt	1/2 c. water
1/2 t. black pepper	3 lbs. chicken pieces
1/2 t. paprika	oil for frying

 In a plastic bag, combine the flour, salt, pepper, paprika, eggs and water. Heat the deep fryer to 355°F according to the manufacturer's instructions. Dip 1 piece of chicken in the batter and allow the excess batter to drip off. Place the chicken in the fryer. Fry 2-3 pieces of chicken at a time, maintaining the proper temperature for optimum results. Fry the chicken about 10 minutes. Using the slotted spoon, turn the chicken pieces and fry for an additional 5-10 minutes, or until the chicken is cooked completely through and is uniformly golden brown. Drain the chicken on absorbent paper and serve warm. Makes 4 servings.

Dill & Onion Battered Fish Fillets

2 c. beer	1 t. salt
2 eggs, beaten	1/2 t. black pepper
1 1/2 c. prepared baking mix	2 lbs. white, mild fish fillets
1 T. fresh dill, finely minced	oil for frying
2 T. white onion, finely minced	prepared malt vinegar
1 clove garlic, finely minced	prepared tartar sauce

 In a large plastic bag, combine the beer, eggs, baking mix, dill, onion, garlic, salt and pepper. Let rest for 20 minutes. Heat the deep fryer to 355°F according to the manufacturer's instructions. Place the fillets in the plastic bag and coat thoroughly with the batter. Deep fry 2-3 fillets at a time for 6-8 minutes, turning once during the frying process. The fillets are done when the fish is cooked through and the batter is golden brown. Repeat with the remaining fillets. Drain the cooked fish on absorbent paper and serve immediately with vinegar or tartar sauce.

Gourmet Lemon Chicken

Lemon Sauce:	1 c. flour
3 T. fresh lemon juice	1 t. baking powder
2 T. sugar	1/2 t. salt
1/2 c. water	3/4 c. water
1 t. cornstarch	1 T. vegetable oil
2 t. water	2 lbs. boneless, skinless chicken breasts
	oil for frying

 In a small saucepan, combine the lemon juice, sugar and ½-cup water. Heat to a boil over medium heat and stir to dissolve the sugar. In a small bowl, combine the cornstarch and water and pour into the boiling lemon and sugar mixture. Reduce the heat to low and stir the sauce until thickened and smooth. Keep warm.

Heat the deep fryer to 355°F according to the manufacturer's instructions. In a large plastic bag, combine the flour, baking powder, salt, water and vegetable oil and mix well to blend. Dip 1 piece of chicken in the batter and allow the excess batter to drip back into the bag. Using a slotted spoon, place the chicken in the fryer and add 1-2 additional pieces of chicken, depending on size. Deep fry until crispy brown and cooked through, about 6-7 minutes. Drain the chicken on absorbent paper and repeat with the remaining chicken pieces. To serve, pour the warm lemon sauce over the cooked chicken. Serves 4-6.

Bayou Fried Catfish

1 c. flour
1/2 t. black pepper
1 t. Cajun seasoning
2 lbs. catfish fillets

2 eggs, beaten
2 c. seasoned breadcrumbs
oil for frying

 Combine the flour, pepper and Cajun seasoning on a large dinner plate. Heat the deep fryer to 340°F according to the manufacturer's instructions. Dredge the fish fillets in the flour and spices. Dip the fillets in the egg and then coat in the breadcrumbs. Place 2-3 fillets in the deep fryer and fry until crispy and brown, about 5-7 minutes. Drain on absorbent paper and serve warm. Serves 4.

County Fair Corn Dogs

1/2 c. cornmeal	1/2 c. buttermilk
1/2 c. flour	3 T. vegetable oil
1 t. salt	1 T. sugar
2 t. baking powder	8 hot dogs
1/2 t. cayenne pepper	oil for frying
1 egg, beaten	8 wooden ice cream sticks or kebob skewers

 In a medium bowl, combine the cornmeal, flour, salt, baking powder and cayenne pepper. Make a well in the center of the dry ingredients and add the egg, buttermilk, oil and sugar. Use a whisk or electric mixer to blend thoroughly.

Heat the deep fryer to 340°F according to the manufacturer's instructions. Place a stick or skewer in one of the small ends of each hot dog. Dip 1 hot dog in the batter, turning to coat completely, and allow the excess batter to drip back into the bowl. Place the corn dog in the deep fryer and repeat the process with 2 additional hot dogs. Fry for 3-4 minutes, or until golden brown and cooked through. Repeat with the remaining corn dogs. Drain on absorbent paper and serve with condiments of your choice. Serves 4.

Quick & Easy Deep-Fried Fish Fillets

1 lb. frozen fish fillets	1 t. salt
2 eggs, beaten	1/2 t. pepper
1 c. flour	1/2 t. paprika
1/2 c. water	oil for frying

 Use fish fillets that are completely frozen; not thawed. Wipe any ice crystals or moisture away from the fillets. Heat the deep fryer to 375°F according to the manufacturer's instructions. Combine the eggs, flour, water, salt, pepper and paprika and blend until smooth. Dip each fillet into the batter and allow the excess batter to drip off. Deep fry the fillets until completely cooked through and crispy, about 8-9 minutes. Serves 4.

Orange Chicken with Wild Rice

2 lbs. boneless, skinless chicken breasts	1 c. seasoned breadcrumbs
2 c. orange juice	1 t. black pepper
1 t. salt	1 t. dried parsley
1/2 t. black pepper	oil for frying
1 clove garlic, finely minced	4-6 c. prepared wild rice, warm
1/2 c. onion, finely minced	1/4 c. slivered almonds
	1 orange, cut into thin slices

 Place the chicken breasts, orange juice, salt, pepper, garlic and onion in a large plastic bag and seal. Refrigerate for at least 2 hours or overnight. Discard the marinade. Heat the deep fryer to 340°F according to the manufacturer's instructions. Combine the breadcrumbs, pepper and parsley on a large dinner plate. Dredge 1 chicken breast in the breadcrumbs and place in the deep fryer. Add 1-2 additional pieces, depending on the space available. Deep fry for 8-10 minutes, turning once. The chicken should be completely cooked through and golden brown when done. Drain on absorbent paper. To serve, mound the wild rice on a warm serving platter. Top with the almond slivers. Add the chicken and garnish with the orange slices. Serves 4-6.

Zesty Italian Fried Chicken

2 eggs, beaten
1 oz. dry Italian salad dressing
   mix
1 c. flour

1/2 t. black pepper
1 T. fresh parsley, minced
3 lbs. chicken pieces
oil for frying

 Place the eggs in a shallow dish. Toss together the salad dressing mix, flour, pepper and parsley on a large dinner plate. Heat the deep fryer to 340°F according to the manufacturer's instructions. Place 1 piece of chicken in the egg and roll in the flour/dressing mixture. Place in the deep fryer and add 1-2 additional pieces of chicken, depending on the size of each piece. Fry for 10-15 minutes, turning once. The chicken is done when completely cooked through and golden brown. Repeat with the remaining pieces. Drain on absorbent paper. Serve immediately. Serves 4.

Classic French-Fried Butterfly Shrimp

1 c. flour

1 t. salt

1/2 t. black pepper

2 eggs, beaten

1 lb. fresh shrimp, cleaned, deveined and split in butterfly fashion

1 c. dry breadcrumbs

oil for frying

 In a medium bowl, combine the flour, salt and pepper. Place the eggs in a shallow dish. Heat the deep fryer to 355°F according to the manufacturer's instructions. To assemble the shrimp, coat each shrimp with the flour, dip in the eggs and roll in the breadcrumbs. Fry 3-5 shrimp for 2 minutes. Turn and fry for 2 minutes, or until cooked through and crispy brown. Drain on absorbent paper and serve immediately. Serves 3-4.

Golden Veal Cutlets with Tomato & Basil Marinara Sauce

Tomato & Basil Marinara Sauce:

8 oz. can tomato sauce

15 oz. can Italian-style stewed tomatoes

1/2 c. fresh parsley, minced

1 c. fresh basil leaves, minced

2 cloves garlic, finely minced

1/4 c. onion, finely minced

1 t. salt

1/2 t. black pepper, freshly ground

1 t. dried Italian seasoning mix

1/2 c. Parmesan cheese, finely shredded

1 c. Italian seasoned breadcrumbs

1/2 t. salt

1/2 t. black pepper

2 lbs. boneless veal cutlets, pounded to 1/4-inch thickness

1 egg, beaten

oil for frying

 Prepare the marinara sauce first by combining the tomato sauce, stewed tomatoes, parsley, basil, garlic, onion, salt, pepper and Italian seasoning in a medium saucepan. Heat over medium until the sauce is simmering. Continue simmering for 30 minutes.

Heat the deep fryer to 340°F according to the manufacturer's instructions. Mix together the seasoned breadcrumbs, salt and pepper on a large dinner plate. To assemble the cutlets, dip each first in the egg then in the breadcrumbs. Place 1-2 cutlets in the deep fryer and fry for 7-9 minutes, or until crispy and brown. Drain on absorbent paper and repeat with the remaining cutlets.

To serve, place the cutlets on a large serving platter. Cover with some of the marinara sauce and garnish with the Parmesan cheese. Pass additional marinara sauce at the table. Serves 4-6.

Homestyle Turkey Pot Pie

1 c. sour cream

1 egg, beaten

3/4 c. milk

1 t. salt

1/2 t. white pepper

1 clove garlic, finely minced

1 small white onion, finely minced

1 c. frozen green peas, thawed
and drained

1 c. carrots, cut into small cubes

1 large potato, peeled and cut
into small cubes

2 c. cooked turkey, shredded

Cheddar Cheese Biscuit Crust:

1 1/2 c. flour

1/4 c. butter or margarine,
softened

3/4 c. buttermilk

1/2 c. cheddar cheese, finely
grated

2 t. baking powder

1/2 t. salt

oil for frying

 Preheat the oven to 375°F. In a large bowl, combine the sour cream, egg, milk, salt and pepper. Blend with an electric mixer or whisk to combine. Add the garlic, onion, peas, carrots, potato and turkey and toss thoroughly to mix well. Spray a 10-inch pie pan with cooking spray and spoon the turkey pie into the pan. Smooth the top with a spatula. Bake the pie for 30 minutes. Place the *Cheddar Cheese Biscuits* on top of the pie, covering as much surface as possible and bake for an additional 5-10 minutes.

To prepare the biscuit crust, heat the deep fryer to 375°F according to the manufacturer's instructions. Cut the butter into the flour using a pastry cutter or two knives. Add the buttermilk and blend. Add the cheese, baking powder and salt and mix for 2 minutes by hand. Carefully drop 3-4 well-rounded tablespoons of dough into the deep fryer and fry for 3-4 minutes, turning once. Remove the biscuits and drain on absorbent paper. Repeat with the remaining biscuits. Use as directed above.

Picnic Basket Fried Chicken

3 c. saltine crackers, finely crushed
1/4 c. dry onion soup mix
3 lbs. chicken pieces
1/2 c. butter or margarine, melted

oil for frying
1 c. prepared barbecue sauce
oil for frying

 Heat the deep fryer to 355°F according to the manufacturer's instructions. Combine the crackers and onion soup mix on a dinner plate. To assemble the chicken for frying, dip 1 piece in the butter and roll in the cracker mixture. Dip the chicken in the egg again and roll in the crackers again. Place the chicken in the fryer and add 1-2 pieces, depending on the space available. Fry for 10-15 minutes, or until completely cooked through and golden brown. Drain on absorbent paper. Serve with barbecue sauce. Serves 4-6.

Chicken-Fried Steak & Zesty New Potatoes

1 c. flour
1 t. salt
1/2 t. black pepper
4 beef cubed steaks

oil for frying
6 new potatoes, cut into wedges 1/4-inch thick
salt & pepper to taste

 Combine the flour, salt and pepper and spread on a large cutting board. Using a meat tenderizer or the edge of a saucer, pound the cubed steaks, turning once in the flour, until they are uniformly ¼-inch thick. Heat the deep fryer to 355°F according to the manufacturer's instructions. Place 1 steak in the fryer and cook for 4-5 minutes, turning once. Remove and drain on absorbent paper. Repeat with the remaining steaks. Place the steaks in a warm oven.

Place 6-8 wedges of potato in the deep fryer and fry for 3-4 minutes, or until golden. Drain on absorbent paper and repeat with the remaining potatoes. Salt and pepper to taste and serve with the steaks. Serves 4.

Buffalo Chicken & Blue Cheese Salad

1 chicken breast, split, skinned and boned

1 c. flour

1 t. salt

1/2 t. black pepper

1/2 t. paprika

10 c. salad greens, torn

2 eggs, hard cooked

2 green onions, thinly sliced

1 large tomato, diced

3 slices bacon, cooked and crumbled

1/4 c. blue cheese, crumbled

1/2 c. prepared blue cheese dressing

 Heat the deep fryer to 355°F according to the manufacturer's instructions. Slice the chicken breast into long, thin strips. Combine the flour, salt, pepper and paprika in a shallow dish. Dredge the chicken in the flour and spices and place 3-4 in the deep fryer. Cook until crispy and cooked through completely, 5-6 minutes. Drain on absorbent paper and repeat with the remaining chicken. Keep the chicken warm while assembling the salads.

Divide the lettuce greens evenly among four individual plates. Layer the eggs, green onions, tomatoes, bacon and blue cheese over each. Plate equal amounts of the fried chicken on top of each salad and drizzle the blue cheese salad dressing over all. Serves 4.

Cowboy Cheeseburgers

1 lb. lean ground beef	2 T. onion, finely minced
1 t. salt	4 oz. American cheese, thinly sliced
1/2 t. black pepper	
1/2 t. garlic powder	4 sesame hamburger buns
1 t. Worcestershire sauce	condiments of your choice
	oil for frying

 Heat the deep fryer to 355°F according to the manufacturer's instructions. In a medium bowl, toss the beef, salt, pepper, garlic powder and Worcestershire sauce to mix. Do not over mix. Add the onion and toss once again. Form the mixture into 8 very thin patties, about 4-inches in diameter. Place cheese slices on each of 4 patties and cover with the remaining 4 patties, sealing the edges of the patties completely. Fry 1-2 patties at a time for 5-8 minutes, or until completely cooked through. Drain on absorbent paper and repeat with the remaining patties. Serve on the sesame hamburger buns with your choice of condiments. Serves 4.

Sunday Night Popcorn Halibut

2 lbs. halibut fillets, cut into 2-inch cubes

1 c. flour

1/2 t. black pepper

1/2 t. salt

1 egg, beaten

1/2 c. beer

1 c. yellow cornmeal

prepared cocktail sauce

oil for frying

Heat the deep fryer to 355°F according to the manufacturer's instructions. Mix the flour with the pepper and salt and pour into a shallow dish. Combine the egg and the beer and beat well. To assemble, dredge each piece of fish in the flour, dip in the egg/beer mixture and roll in the cornmeal. Fry 3-5 pieces at a time for 5-6 minutes, turning to brown evenly. Drain on absorbent paper and repeat with the remaining fillets. Serve with the cocktail sauce. Serves 6.

CHAPTER FIVE

Vegetables & Side Dishes

Although cooks may not typically think about using a deep fryer when preparing vegetables, the results are surprisingly delicious! Quick cooking at high heat maintains the bright colors and natural vitamins and minerals of vegetables. If you have not tried deep-fried vegetables before, consider preparing the *Crispy Battered Vegetables Potpourri* recipe first. The light and mild batter coating truly accompanies robust vegetables very nicely and can be paired with a variety of sauces and other side dishes.

Sometimes the most attractive part of your meal may be a side dish that accents a fairly simple cut of meat. Consider light and flavorful *Herbed Eggplant Slices* or *Fried Shrimp & Baby Greens Salad*. For heartier appetites, choose *French-Fried Potato Wedges* or *Deep-Fried Potato Salad*. And, for elegant dinners, you may want to select *Dill Fried Shallots* or *Winter Asparagus*. Keep your deep fryer handy for exciting vegetables and side dishes any night of the week!

Fried Spinach

1 egg, beaten

1 c. milk

1 c. flour

1 t. salt

1/2 t. white pepper

1/8 t. paprika

20 spinach leaves, cleaned and dried, tough ends removed

oil for frying

 In a medium bowl, combine the egg, milk, flour, salt, pepper and paprika. Blend well with a whisk or electric mixer. Heat the deep fryer to 355°F according to the manufacturer's instructions. Dip 1 spinach leaf into the batter and allow the excess to drip back into the bowl. Place the spinach leaf in the fryer. Add 2-3 additional leaves, depending on the space available in the fryer. Fry for 2-3 minutes, or until the batter is golden brown. Drain the leaves on absorbent paper and repeat with the remaining leaves. Serves 4.

Homestyle Potato Chips

4 Russet potatoes, skins removed   salt and pepper to taste
oil for frying

 Using a mandoline or food slicer, slice the potatoes into paper-thin pieces. Place in a large bowl of water for 1 hour. Drain and completely dry the potato slices. Heat the deep fryer to 375°F according to the manufacturer's instructions. Place a handful of potatoes in the fryer and cook for 1-2 minutes. Turn and fry for 1 minute. Chips should be lightly browned and crispy when done. Remove and drain the chips on absorbent paper. Repeat with the remaining chips. Salt to taste while warm. Makes about 5 cups of potato chips.

Crispy Battered Vegetables Potpourri

1 1/2 c. flour

2 t. baking powder

1/2 oz. ranch salad dressing mix

1 1/2 c. beer

2 eggs, beaten

4 c. assorted vegetables of your choice—broccoli florets, cauliflower, baby mushrooms, sliced zucchini, sliced or cubed carrots, etc.

oil for frying

soy sauce

In a large bowl, combine the flour, baking powder, ranch dressing mix, beer and eggs. Mix well until completely blended. Heat the deep fryer to 355°F according to the manufacturer's instructions. Cut the vegetables into uniform sizes (this will ensure that the vegetables cook for the same duration). To assemble, dip 3-6 pieces of vegetable into the batter and then place in the deep fryer. Add vegetables if space allows. Fry the vegetables for 3-4 minutes, turning once. Drain on absorbent paper and repeat with the remaining vegetables. Serve immediately with soy sauce, if desired. Makes 4 servings.

Herbed Eggplant Slices

1/2 t. salt
1/2 t. black pepper
1 c. flour
1/4 t. ground oregano
1/4 t. ground basil

1/4 t. onion powder
1 eggplant, peeled and sliced in
1/2-inch pieces
2 eggs, beaten
oil for frying

 In a shallow, wide dish combine the salt, pepper, flour, oregano, basil and thyme. Toss with a fork to mix. Heat the deep fryer to 340°F according to the manufacturer's instructions. Dip each eggplant slice in the eggs and then in the flour and herbs, turning once to coat. Fry 1-2 slices of eggplant at a time, turning once, for about 5 minutes. The slices will be golden brown when done. Makes 4 servings.

Southern Corn Fritters

1 c. flour

1 t. baking powder

1 t. salt

1/2 t. black pepper

1/4 t. cayenne pepper

1 egg, beaten

15 oz. can creamed corn

oil for frying

powdered sugar to taste

 In a large bowl, combine the flour, baking powder, salt, black pepper and cayenne pepper. Blend well. Add the egg and creamed corn and mix thoroughly. Heat the deep fryer to 340°F according to the manufacturer's instructions. Carefully drop rounded tablespoons of the corn fritter mix into the oil, frying 2-3 fritters at a time. Fry for 2 minutes and turn once. Fry for 2 minutes. Remove the fritters from the fryer basket and drain on absorbent paper. Repeat with the remaining fritter batter. Dust with powdered sugar just before serving, if desired. Serves 4.

French-Fried Potato Wedges

6 baking potatoes, peeled and cut
   into 8 wedges each

oil for frying

salt and pepper to taste

 Place the potato wedges in a large bowl, cover with water and a pinch of salt and set aside for 1 hour. Remove the potatoes from the water and pat dry with paper towels. Heat the deep fryer to 375°F according to the manufacturer's instructions. Place 6-8 wedges in the deep fryer and fry for 2-3 minutes, or until cooked through and golden brown. Drain on absorbent paper and repeat with the remaining potato wedges. Add salt and pepper to taste just before serving. Serves 4.

Sweet Potato 'n' Nutmeg Fries

4 sweet potatoes
oil for frying
3 T. brown sugar

2 t. salt
1 t. ground nutmeg

 Boil the potatoes for 15 minutes. Remove from the heat and peel. Cut the potatoes into thin strips for fries. Heat the deep fryer to 375°F according to the manufacturer's instructions. Place a handful of potatoes in the fryer and cook for 2-3 minutes or until browned. Turn and fry for 1 minute. Remove and drain on absorbent paper. Repeat with the remaining potatoes. Before serving, mix together the brown sugar, salt and nutmeg and sprinkle over the fries. Serve while warm. Serves 4.

Friday Night Onion Rings

6 large sweet onions, peeled	1 t. black pepper
2 c. flour	2 c. milk
1/4 c. yellow cornmeal	2 eggs, beaten
2 T. onion powder	oil for frying
2 t. salt	

 Slice the onions into ½-inch thick rounds and separate the rings. Place the rings in a very large bowl of ice water for 5 minutes. Drain and dry each onion ring completely. In a large bowl, combine the flour, cornmeal, onion powder, salt and pepper. Mix well. Add the milk and eggs and beat again.

Heat the deep fryer to 355°F according to the manufacturer's instructions. Dip 1 onion ring in the batter and allow the excess to drip back into the bowl. Place the onion ring in the deep fryer and add 4-5 additional battered onion rings, if space allows. Fry for 2 minutes. Turn and fry for 1-2 minutes. Drain the onion rings on absorbent paper and repeat with the remaining onion rings. Serves 4-6.

Mexican Tomato & Onion Salsa Fritters

1 c. flour
1 t. baking powder
1 t. salt
1/2 t. black pepper
1/4 t. chili powder
2 eggs, beaten

1 large, ripe tomato, chopped
1/2 c. white onion, chopped
1 T. fresh cilantro, finely minced
1 t. garlic, minced
oil for frying

 In a large bowl, combine the flour, baking powder, black pepper and chili powder. Mix well. Add the eggs, tomato, onion, cilantro and garlic and mix again. Heat the deep fryer to 340°F according to the manufacturer's instructions. Drop the fritters by rounded tablespoons into the hot oil. Fry 2-3 fritters at a time for 4 minutes, turning once. Drain on absorbent paper and repeat with the remaining fritters. Serves 4.

Baby Red Potatoes & Sour Cream Sauce

12 small red potatoes, scrubbed and halved

oil for frying

Sour Cream Sauce:

1 c. dairy sour cream

1/2 t. salt

1/2 t. black pepper, freshly ground

2 T. chives, finely minced

2 T. sweet onions, finely minced

parsley sprigs for garnish

 Prepare the potatoes by scooping out the centers of each half, leaving a small edge around each shell. Heat the deep fryer to 355°F according to the manufacturer's instructions. Deep fry the potato shells for 3-4 minutes each and drain on absorbent paper. While the potatoes cool, combine the sour cream, salt, pepper, chives and onion. Spoon the *Sour Cream Sauce* into the potato shells, garnish with tiny sprigs of parsley and serve immediately. Serves 4.

Parmesan & Zucchini Fritters

1/2 c. prepared baking mix
1/2 t. salt
1/4 t. black pepper
1/2 c. Parmesan cheese, finely
  grated

2 eggs, beaten
2 c. fresh zucchini, finely grated
  and squeezed dry
oil for frying

 Heat the deep fryer to 355°F according to the manufacturer's instructions. In a large bowl, combine the baking mix, salt, pepper, Parmesan cheese, eggs and zucchini. Blend well. Drop the batter by a rounded tablespoon into the deep fryer. Add 2-3 additional fritters and cook for 4 minutes. Turn the fritters once to evenly coat both sides. Drain on absorbent paper and repeat with the remaining batter. Serves 4.

Winter Asparagus

2 lbs. fresh asparagus	1/2 t. black pepper
1 c. flour	3/4 c. beer
1/2 c. cornstarch	2 egg whites, beaten to stiff
1 t. baking powder	peaks
1 t. salt	oil for frying

 Remove the woody ends of each stalk of asparagus. Clean and dry the stalks thoroughly. Set aside. In a large bowl, combine the flour, cornstarch, baking powder, salt, pepper and beer. Use a whisk or electric mixer to blend completely. Fold in the egg whites. Heat the deep fryer to 340°F according to the manufacturer's instructions. Dip 1 stalk of asparagus in the batter and allow the excess batter to drip off. Using a slotted spoon, place the stalk in the deep fryer. Repeat with 2-3 stalks, depending on the space in the deep fryer. Fry the asparagus for 1 minute. Turn and fry for an additional minute, or until the asparagus is golden brown. Serve while warm. Makes 4 servings.

Fried Shrimp & Baby Greens Salad

18 medium, uncooked shrimp, deveined and tails removed

2 c. saltine crackers, finely crushed

1/2 t. salt

1/2 t. black pepper

1 egg, beaten

oil for frying

12 c. assorted baby greens of your choice, washed and shredded

1 small jicama, peeled and cut into matchsticks

1 c. canned corn kernels, drained

1 large beefsteak tomato, cut into thin wedges

1 Serrano chili, seeded and minced fine

1 small tomato, chopped

1/4 c. onion, chopped

2 cloves garlic, chopped

2 T. fresh cilantro, chopped

1/4 c. sesame oil

2 T. rice vinegar

1/2 c. water

salt and pepper to taste

 Cut each shrimp into 3 pieces. On a large plate, combine the cracker crumbs, salt and pepper. Heat the deep fryer to 355°F according to the manufacturer's instructions. Dip each piece of shrimp in the egg and roll in the crumb mixture. Place 8-10 pieces of shrimp in the deep fryer and cook for 2 minutes. Turn and cook for 1 minute. Remove from the fryer and drain on absorbent paper. Repeat with the remaining shrimp. Keep warm in a 200°F oven.

Prepare the salad by combining the baby greens, jicama, tomato and corn in a large serving bowl. Prepare the dressing by blending in a blender or food processor the chili, tomato, onion, garlic, cilantro, oil, vinegar and water. Blend until smooth and add salt and pepper to taste.

To assemble the salad, place the fried shrimp over the greens and vegetables. Drizzle the salad dressing over all to taste. Serve immediately. Serves 6.

Louisiana Fried Green Tomatoes

6 green tomatoes, cut in 1/4-inch
   slices

1 c. yellow cornmeal

2 c. flour

1 t. salt

1/2 t. white pepper

2 1/4 c. milk

oil for frying

 Place the tomato slices on paper towels to drain the excess juices. In a large bowl, combine the cornmeal, flour, salt, pepper and milk. Blend until smooth and thick. Heat the deep fryer to 340°F according to the manufacturer's instructions. Dip 1 tomato slice in the batter and allow the excess to drip back into the bowl. (Less coating results in a better texture.) Carefully place the tomato slice in the fryer and add 1-2 additional slices as directed, depending on space in the fryer. Fry the tomatoes for 2 minutes. Turn and fry for 1 minute. Remove from the fryer and stand the slices upright in a colander to drain. Repeat the process with the remaining tomato slices. Serves 6-8.

Deep-Fried Valley Artichokes

6 small artichokes, outer leaves removed, cut into quarters

1 c. flour

2 eggs, beaten

2 c. sourdough bread crumbs

oil for frying

 Using a large saucepan or stockpot, blanch the artichokes in boiling water for 8 minutes. Remove the artichokes from the water and rinse with cool water. Drain and separate the leaves gently on each artichoke quarter without breaking the leaves from the heart. Dry the artichokes with paper towels.

Heat the deep fryer to 320°F according to the manufacturer's instructions. Dip 1 artichoke in the flour to cover completely. Shake off the excess. Dip the artichoke in the egg. Coat the artichoke with the bread crumbs. Place the artichoke in the deep fryer. Repeat with 3-4 additional pieces. Fry the artichokes for 2 minutes. Turn and fry for 1-2 minutes. Remove and drain on absorbent paper. Repeat with the remaining artichokes and serve while warm. Serves 6.

Blue Ribbon Corn-on-the-Cob

6 ears fresh corn on the cob, husks and silk removed

oil for frying

1/2 c. butter, melted

salt and pepper to taste

 Heat the deep fryer to 300°F according to the manufacturer's instructions. Dry each ear of corn thoroughly. Place 1 ear of corn in the fryer and cook for 3 minutes. Do not overcook or allow the corn to turn brown. Remove the corn from the fryer and drain on absorbent paper. Repeat with the remaining ears of corn. To serve, brush each ear with melted butter and salt and pepper lightly. Serves 6.

Note: You may substitute frozen corn on the cob. Thaw the corn completely and pat dry. Fry each ear of corn for 3-4 minutes.

Deep-Fried Parsley

2 bunches fresh parsley
1 c. seasoned bread crumbs
1/2 t. salt
1/4 t. black pepper

1/2 c. flour
1 egg, beaten
oil for frying

 Cut the lower stems from the parsley and gather into small bunches. Use a paper towel to remove any moisture from the parsley. In a small bowl, mix the bread crumbs with the salt and pepper. Heat the deep fryer to 340°F according to the manufacturer's instructions. To assemble the parsley, dip 1 small bunch in the flour, then in the egg. Roll the bunch in the bread crumbs. Place in the deep fryer and add 1-2 additional bunches. Fry for 1 minute, turning once. Drain on absorbent paper and repeat with the remaining parsley bunches. Serves 4-6.

Fried Cauliflower with Zippy Cheese Sauce

1 large cauliflower, broken into florets and blanched until tender-crisp

1 c. flour

1 t. salt

1/2 t. black pepper

1/2 t. baking powder

3/4 c. beer

oil for frying

Zippy Cheese Sauce:

2 T. butter or margarine

2 T. flour

1/4 t. white pepper

1/2 t. cayenne pepper

1 c. milk

1 c. cheddar cheese, shredded

Drain the cauliflower and pat dry with paper towels. In a medium bowl, combine the flour, salt, pepper, baking powder and beer. Mix well until smooth. Heat the deep fryer to 340°F according to the manufacturer's instructions. Dip 1 cauliflower floret in the batter and place in the deep fryer. Add 5-7 florets, as space allows. Fry for 5 minutes. Turn and fry for 2-3 additional minutes, or until cooked through and golden brown. Drain on absorbent paper. Serve with *Zippy Cheese Sauce*. Makes 4 servings.

To prepare the *Zippy Cheese Sauce*, heat the butter and flour in a medium saucepan, stirring constantly.

Add the peppers and slowly add the milk, stirring constantly. Bring the sauce to a boil, reduce the heat and add the cheddar cheese. Stir until thick and smooth. Serve immediately with the fried cauliflower.

Dill Fried Shallots

8 medium shallots, peeled and halved

1 c. seasoned bread crumbs

1 T. fresh dill weed, finely minced

1/4 t. black pepper

1 egg, beaten

oil for frying

Blanch the shallots in boiling water for 4 minutes. Remove and pat dry. Heat the deep fryer to 355°F according to the manufacturer's instructions. In a shallow bowl, combine the bread crumbs, dill weed and black pepper. Dip 1 shallot half in the egg and roll in the bread crumb mixture. Place in the deep fryer. Add 2-3 additional shallots, depending on space, and fry for 3 minutes. Turn and fry for 2 minutes, or until cooked through and crispy. Drain on absorbent paper and repeat with the remaining shallots. Serves 4.

Deep-Fried Potato Salad with Tomato Tarragon Dressing

3 large Russet potatoes, peeled and cubed in 1/2-inch pieces

oil for frying

1/2 c. water chestnuts, slivered

1/4 c. green onions, thinly sliced

3 hard-cooked eggs, roughly chopped

1 c. frozen green peas, cooked and drained

Tomato Tarragon Dressing:

1 medium tomato, peeled

1/4 c. mayonnaise

3 T. tarragon vinegar (apple cider vinegar may be substituted)

1 T. fresh tarragon, finely minced

1/2 c. dairy sour cream

salt and pepper to taste

ground paprika

 Heat the deep fryer to 375°F according to the manufacturer's instructions. Deep fry the potato cubes in batches for 2-3 minutes and drain on absorbent paper. Keep warm. In a large salad bowl, assemble the water chestnuts, green onions, eggs and peas. Toss to combine. Prepare the *Tomato Tarragon Dressing* by processing in a blender the tomato, mayonnaise, vinegar, tarragon, sour cream, salt and pepper. When smooth, pour over the vegetables and eggs. Add the fried potatoes and toss lightly once again. Sprinkle with the paprika. Serve immediately. Serves 4.

Chinese Chicken & Pineapple Salad

3 boneless, skinless chicken breast halves

1 c. pineapple juice

1 c. fresh pineapple, cut into small chunks

1/2 c. fresh papaya, cut into small chunks

1/4 c. red bell pepper, diced

2 T. fresh parsley, minced

2 green onions, sliced

8 c. mixed greens of your choice

10 square wonton wrappers, thinly sliced

oil for frying

1/2 c. pineapple juice

2 T. sesame oil

2 T. rice wine vinegar

1/2 t. salt

1/4 t. freshly ground black pepper

1/4 c. slivered almonds

 Use an indoor or outdoor grill to cook the chicken breasts for 8 minutes. Baste the chicken lightly with 1 cup of the pineapple juice. The chicken should be cooked through completely when done. Remove from the grill and shred. Set aside.

In a large bowl, combine the pineapple, papaya, red bell pepper, parsley, green onions and mixed greens. Heat the deep fryer to 375°F according to the manufacturer's instructions. Fry the sliced wontons for 2 minutes, stirring to separate the thin strips. Remove to absorbent paper and drain.

Prepare the dressing by combining in a shaker the ½ cup pineapple juice, sesame oil, vinegar, salt and pepper. Shake vigorously. To assemble the salad, divide the greens and pineapple mixture among four individual plates. Scatter the chicken over each plate evenly. Lightly dress each salad and top with the wonton strips. Sprinkle each serving with the almonds. Serve immediately. Serves 4.

Margarita Tortilla Salad

6 small corn tortillas, cut into 1/4-inch thick strips

oil for frying

10 c. torn salad greens, washed

1 c. canned black beans, drained

1 c. canned corn kernels, drained

1 clove garlic, finely minced

3 green onions, finely sliced

2 firm tomatoes, chopped

1/2 c. black olives, sliced

Margarita Dressing:

2 T. prepared margarita mix (with or without alcohol)

1/2 c. extra virgin olive oil

2 T. water

1/2 t. salt

1/2 t. black pepper

1/4 t. chili powder

Heat the deep fryer to 375°F according to the manufacturer's instructions. Fry the tortilla strips in small batches for 2-3 minutes or until crispy and golden brown. Remove from the fryer and drain on absorbent paper.

In a large salad bowl, assemble the greens, black beans, corn, garlic, onions, tomatoes and olives. Toss well. Prepare the salad dressing by whisking together the margarita mix, olive oil, water, salt, black pepper and chili powder. Dress the salad to taste. Divide the tortilla strips evenly among 4 individual plates. Top with even portions of the salad. Serve immediately. Serves 4.

CHAPTER SIX

Specialties From Around the World

As today's technology removes the boundaries of our world, the gates open wide for exploring the tastes and textures of other cultures. And what a delight it is! In the past few decades we've experienced many new and creative types of fare from countries including India, Russia, the Far East, Africa and South America. Because of this surge of interest, we've now adapted and adopted delicious dishes and many of these call for the use of a deep fryer.

Inside this chapter you'll find many recipes to try when you are looking for a fun meal. Whether you choose to experiment with your family or perhaps with a group of friends, you'll find that each of these has flavors and textures that are inviting for everyone. Try *Ranchero*

Mexican Chimichangas or *Spicy Pork & Shrimp Lumpias* with your family. For dinner guests, choose *Deep-Fried Ravioli with Rich Tomato Sauce* or *Japanese Surf & Turf Tempura*. And be prepared for exciting new cuisine journeys!

Deep-Fried Italian Ravioli with Rich Tomato Sauce

16 oz. frozen cheese ravioli

oil for frying

14 oz. can plum tomatoes, drained and chopped

2 T. extra virgin olive oil

8 oz. can tomato sauce

1 t. salt

1/2 t. black pepper

1 t. ground oregano

1 medium onion, chopped

2 cloves garlic, minced

1 green pepper, seeded and minced

 Heat the deep fryer to 355°F according to the manufacturer's instructions. Carefully place 8-10 ravioli in the deep fryer, using a slotted spoon. Fry each for about 2 minutes, or until cooked through and crispy. Remove and drain on absorbent paper. Repeat with the remaining ravioli. Keep the fried ravioli warm on an ovenproof plate in the oven at 200°F.

In a large saucepan, combine the tomatoes, olive oil, tomato sauce, salt, pepper, oregano, onion, garlic and green pepper. Heat, stirring occasionally until the sauce is bubbling. Reduce the heat and simmer for 20 minutes over very low heat.

To assemble the ravioli, pour the sauce over the fried ravioli. Pass with shredded Parmesan cheese, if desired. Serves 4.

Ranchero Mexican Chimichangas

1 lb. lean ground beef	1/2 t. salt
1 medium white onion, chopped	6 large flour tortillas
1 T. flour	oil for frying
1 T. butter	1 c. dairy sour cream
1 c. water	2 c. Pepper Jack cheese, shredded
4 oz. canned tomato sauce	2 c. green lettuce, finely chopped
2 T. chili powder seasoning	1/4 c. green onions, finely chopped

 In a medium pan, sauté the beef with the onion and drain any grease from the meat. In a small saucepan, combine the butter and flour and heat until thickened. Gradually add the water until the sauce is thickened and smooth. Add the tomato sauce. Blend in the chili powder and salt and stir well. Keep warm over low heat.

Heat the deep fryer to 340°F according to the manufacturer's instructions. To assemble the chimichangas, layer the beef and onion and 2 tablespoons of the sauce in each tortilla. Fold in the ends of the tortilla and roll tightly. Place 1 chimichanga in the deep fryer and fry for 1-2 minutes. Turn and fry 2 minutes. Remove from the fryer, drain on absorbent paper and keep warm while frying the remaining chimichangas. To serve, garnish each chimichanga with sour cream, Pepper Jack cheese, lettuce and green onions. Serves 4.

Caribbean Seafood Fried Wraps with Creamy Dill Dressing

1 lb. fresh shrimp (you may substitute frozen, thawed shrimp)

1 lb. fresh crabmeat (you may substitute canned crabmeat)

2 T. sesame oil

1/4 c. green onion, finely chopped

1/4 c. white onion, finely chopped

1 red bell pepper, finely chopped

2 medium tomatoes, chopped

2 T. fresh cilantro, finely minced

salt and pepper to taste

6 large flour tortillas

oil for frying

Creamy Dill Dressing

1 c. dairy sour cream

1/2 c. mayonnaise

2 t. fresh dill weed, minced

1/2 t. salt

1/4 t. white pepper

pinch chili powder

In a large sauté pan, cook the shrimp and crabmeat in the vegetable oil over medium heat for 3 minutes. Add the green onion, white onion, red pepper, tomatoes, cilantro and salt and pepper and sauté for an additional 2 minutes.

Heat the deep fryer to 340°F according to the manufacturer's instructions. To assemble the wraps, place 1 tortilla on a flat surface and scoop 2 large tablespoons of seafood and vegetables onto the center portion of the tortilla. Fold under both ends and wrap the tortilla lengthwise completely, enclosing the seafood filling. Deep fry the wrap for 2-3 minutes, turning once and frying again for 2-3 minutes to brown on both sides. Drain on absorbent paper and repeat with the remaining wraps.

To assemble the *Creamy Dill Dressing*, combine in a small bowl the sour cream, mayonnaise, dill weed, salt, pepper and chili powder. Refrigerate until ready to use. Offer the dressing at the table with the wraps. Serves 6.

Japanese Surf & Turf Tempura

1 egg

1 c. cold water

1 c. flour

1/4 t. baking powder

1/4 t. salt

oil for frying

1 lb. sirloin steak, cut into 1-inch pieces

1/2 lb. fresh lobster, cut into 1-inch pieces

1/2 lb. fresh shrimp, deveined and tails removed

6 c. prepared jasmine rice, warm

Oriental fish sauce to taste

soy sauce to taste

In a medium bowl, beat the egg with an electric mixer for 2 minutes. Add the cold water and beat again. Slowly add the flour, baking powder and salt and continue mixing for 2 minutes. Heat the deep fryer to 340°F according to the manufacturer's instructions. Assemble the steak, lobster and shrimp. Dip 2-3 pieces of meat or seafood in the tempura batter and allow the excess to drip back into the bowl. Place the pieces in the deep fryer and fry 3-4 minutes or until cooked through and golden brown. Drain on absorbent paper. Repeat with the remaining pieces of steak and seafood. Serve immediately with the jasmine rice and pass the sauces at the table. Serves 4.

Yucatan Tostada Salad

6 large corn tortillas	2 c. chicken, cooked and shredded
3 small corn tortillas, cut into 1/4-inch slices	2 c. prepared medium tomato salsa
oil for frying	1 c. Jack cheese, shredded
8 c. mixed greens, shredded	1/2 c. dairy sour cream
2 c. canned black beans, drained	1/4 c. green onion, finely sliced
1 c. canned corn kernels, drained	prepared taco sauce

Heat the deep fryer to 375°F according to the manufacturer's instructions. Place 1 tortilla in the hot oil. Quickly push down on the tortilla with the base of a large can, creating a bowl-like indentation in the tortilla. Fry until crisp, about 2-3 minutes. Carefully remove the tortilla and drain on absorbent paper. Repeat with the remaining 5 tortillas. Cook small batches of the 3 sliced tortillas in the hot oil and drain on absorbent paper.

To assemble the salads, place 1 tortilla shell on each of 6 individual plates. Place 2 cups of lettuce inside each shell. Layer the beans, corn, chicken and salsa equally on each tortilla. Top with the Jack cheese and garnish each salad with sour cream and green onions. Pass the taco sauce at the table. Serves 6.

Spicy Pork & Shrimp Lumpias

1 lb. medium shrimp, cleaned and tails removed

1 lb. pork, thinly sliced

2 T. soy sauce

1 T. sesame oil

1 t. ground ginger

2 cloves garlic, finely minced

1/2 c. green onions, thinly sliced

1 t. salt

1/2 t. black pepper

1/2 c. carrots, cut into pieces about 1-inch long and 1/4-inch wide

1 c. bean sprouts, cleaned and drained and cut into 1-inch pieces

12 wonton or lumpia wrappers

oil for frying

 In a large saucepan, sauté the shrimp and pork in the soy sauce and oil. Add the ground ginger, garlic and green onions and heat for 1 minute. Add the salt, pepper, carrots and bean sprouts and cook for an additional 1 minute. Remove from the heat.

To assemble the lumpia, place 1 wrapper on a flat surface. Spoon about 2 tablespoons of lumpia filling down the center of the wrapper. Fold in the short ends of the wrapper and wrap the longer ends around, completely enclosing the filling. Use a bit of water to seal the edges of the lumpia. Repeat with the remaining wrappers and filling.

Heat the deep fryer to 355°F according to the manufacturer's instructions. Fry 2 lumpia for 2 minutes. Turn and fry for 2 minutes, or until evenly browned and crispy. Remove and drain on absorbent paper. Repeat with the remaining lumpia. Makes 12 appetizers or 3 entrées.

Asian Lamb Dumplings

Lamb Filling:
1/4 c. vegetable oil
1 T. flour
1 lb. lean ground lamb
2 T. fresh cilantro, finely minced
1 T. fresh parsley, finely minced
2 t. salt
1 t. black pepper
1 egg, beaten

1/4 c. long-grain rice, cooked and cooled

Dumpling Dough:
4 c. flour
1 t. salt
3 eggs
1 c. warm water
oil for frying

 Combine the oil, flour, lamb, cilantro, parsley, salt, pepper and rice. Set aside. Prepare the dumpling dough by combining the flour and salt in a large bowl. Mix well. Add the eggs and water and mix together until the dough leaves the sides of the bowl and can be made into a ball. Add up to an additional ½ cup of flour, if needed. Turn the dough onto a lightly floured board and knead for 5-10 minutes, until the dough is smooth and elastic. Using a floured rolling pin, roll the dough until the dough is very thin and you can almost see the surface underneath the dough. Use a floured cookie cutter or glass to cut 3-inch circles from the dough.

Place 1 heaping tablespoon of the lamb filling on one-half of the dough circles. Top with the remaining dough circles. Lightly moisten the edges of each piece of dough with the beaten egg and crimp the edges with a fork to completely seal.

Heat the deep fryer to 355°F according to the manufacturer's instructions. Place 5-6 dumplings in the deep fryer and cook for 2-3 minutes, or until golden brown and completely cooked. Drain on absorbent paper and repeat with the remaining dumplings. Serve immediately. Makes 4 entrée servings or 12 appetizer servings.

Spicy Italian Parmesan & Pork Tarts

Italian Tart Dough:

1/4 oz. active dry yeast

1 c. warm water (110-115°F)

1 t. sugar

1 t. salt

1/2 t. ground oregano

6-7 c. flour

1 c. milk

3 T. extra virgin olive oil

2 T. dry white wine

Parmesan & Pork Filling:

1 egg, beaten

1/4 c. Italian-seasoned bread crumbs

1/2 lb. lean ground pork

1/2 c. Parmesan cheese, finely shredded

1/4 c. fresh parsley, minced

1/2 t. crushed red pepper

1/2 t. ground oregano

1 t. black pepper

1 t. salt

oil for frying

In a small bowl, combine the yeast, water and sugar. Stir until the yeast is dissolved. In a large bowl, mix together the yeast/water mixture with 2 cups of flour. Make a smooth batter by blending vigorously. Add up to 5 cups of flour, alternating the flour with the milk, oil and wine. The dough should leave the sides of the bowl when done. Using a floured board, knead the dough for 5-10 minutes, until smooth and elastic. Place in a greased bowl, turn, and cover with a clean cloth. Let rise for 1½ to 2 hours, or until doubled in size. Punch down the dough and make small balls, about the size of walnuts. Place the balls on a clean surface and allow to rise again for 45 minutes.

Prepare the filling by mixing together the egg, bread crumbs, pork, Parmesan cheese, parsley, red pepper, oregano, pepper and salt. Mix by hand until all ingredients are well-incorporated.

To assemble the tarts, use a rolling pin to roll out each ball of dough into a 3-4 inch circle. Place 1 heaping tablespoon on the pork mixture on 1 side of the circle and fold the other half over the top. Seal the edges of the dough with a bit of water around the edges. Crimp with a fork. Heat the deep fryer to 355°F according to the manufacturer's instructions. Using a slotted spoon, place 4-6 tarts in the fryer and cook for 5-6 minutes, or until the tarts are golden brown and the meat filling is completely cooked inside. Repeat with the remaining tarts. Drain on absorbent paper. Makes 4-6 servings.

Italian Fried Cheese

1 1/2 c. ricotta cheese, drained	2 eggs, separated
1 c. Parmesan cheese, finely shredded	1 c. Italian-seasoned bread crumbs
2 T. fresh parsley, finely minced	oil for frying
1 T. fresh chives, finely minced	2 c. prepared marinara sauce
1 clove garlic, finely minced	

 In a medium bowl, combine the ricotta cheese, Parmesan cheese, parsley, chives and garlic. Mix well to blend completely. Form the mixture into small (2-inch) bars. Heat the deep fryer to 355°F according to the manufacturer's instructions. Roll 1 cheese bar in the beaten eggs. Roll the bar in the seasoned bread crumbs. Dip the cheese in the egg again and roll in the crumbs again. Place 4-6 bars in the fryer and fry for 3 minutes, or until crispy and browned. To serve, pass the marinara sauce at the table. Serves 4.

Thai Cilantro Noodle Salad

4 oz. rice vermicelli	2 carrots, finely chopped
oil for frying	2 T. sesame oil
2 green onions, thinly sliced	1 T. mayonnaise
1 clove garlic, minced	1/2 c. plain yogurt
1 c. bean sprouts, cleaned and cut into 1-inch pieces	1/4 t. cayenne pepper
	1 T. mirin (sweet rice wine)
2 T. fresh cilantro, minced	2 T. soy sauce

Heat the deep fryer to 375°F according to the manufacturer's instructions. Using a slotted spoon, place about one-fourth of the rice vermicelli in the fryer and cook for 1 minute, or until very lightly browned. Drain on absorbent paper and repeat with the remaining vermicelli. Set aside to cool slightly.

To assemble the salad, combine the green onions, garlic, bean sprouts, cilantro and carrots in a large serving bowl. In a small bowl, mix together the sesame oil, mayonnaise, yogurt, cayenne pepper, mirin and soy sauce. Whisk thoroughly to blend. To present the salads, place equal portions of the vermicelli on 4 plates. Top with the vegetables and pour the dressing over each serving. Makes 4 servings.

Malaysian Shrimp Noodle Bowl

8 oz. firm tofu, cut into small cubes and dried

oil for frying

1 T. vegetable oil

2 eggs, beaten

2 T. sesame oil

1/2 lb. shrimp, peeled and deveined

1 T. sesame oil

1 clove garlic, minced

1/2 t. cayenne pepper

2 T. chili sauce

6 oz. thin rice vermicelli, soaked and drained

3 c. fresh bean sprouts, cleaned and cut into 2-inch lengths

3 green onions, thinly sliced

1/4 c. oyster sauce

1/4 t. black pepper

Heat the deep fryer to 375°F according to the manufacturer's instructions. Fry the tofu cubes, a handful at a time, for 3-4 minutes. Drain on absorbent paper and repeat with the remaining tofu cubes. Heat 1 tablespoon of vegetable oil in a large sauté pan. Add the eggs and swirl the pan to distribute the eggs and cook in omelet-style. Cool the eggs and slice thinly.

Using the same sauté pan, heat 2 tablespoons of sesame oil and add the shrimp, garlic, cayenne pepper and chili sauce. Cook over medium for 2 minutes. Add the vermicelli noodles, bean sprouts, green onions, oyster sauce and pepper and toss until well combined. Add the tofu cubes and eggs and heat just until all ingredients are warm. Serve immediately. Serves 4.

Italian Fried Zeppole

1/4 oz. pkg. active dry yeast	2 T. white wine
1 c. water (110-115°F)	oil for frying
1 1/2 c. flour	powdered sugar
1/2 t. salt	

 Dissolve the yeast in the water in a small bowl. In a medium bowl, combine the flour, salt and white wine. Add the yeast and water mixture and mix well. Turn the dough onto a lightly floured board and knead for 10 minutes, or until the dough is smooth and satiny. Place the dough in a bowl that has been greased with vegetable oil and turn. Cover with a clean cloth and let rise in a warm place for 1-1½ hours.

Heat the deep fryer to 375°F according to the manufacturer's instructions. Pull small pieces of the dough (about the size of a large walnut) and drop into the oil. Fry 5-6 pieces at a time, turning once to brown. Drain on absorbent paper and repeat with the remaining dough. Makes 12-15 fried breads.

Singapore Crab Salad

8 oz. rice vermicelli

oil for frying

1/2 lb. fresh crabmeat

1 clove garlic, finely minced

1 red chili, finely minced

2 t. fresh ginger, grated

2 green onions, thinly sliced

1 carrot, grated

1 c. sliced cucumbers

1 c. fresh bean sprouts, cut into 1-inch pieces

1/2 c. fresh mint leaves, minced

1 T. fresh basil, minced

Crab Dressing

2 T. Oriental fish sauce

2 T. lime juice

1 T. sesame oil

2 T. soy sauce

1 T. rice wine vinegar

2 t. brown sugar

1 T. garlic, minced

Heat the deep fryer to 375°F according to the manufacturer's instructions. Fry the vermicelli in small portions until lightly browned. Drain on absorbent paper and set aside.

In a large mixing bowl, combine the crab, chili, ginger, green onions, carrot, cucumbers, bean sprouts, mint and basil. Toss well. Prepare the *Crab Dressing* by combining in a blender the fish sauce, lime juice, sesame oil, soy sauce, vinegar, brown sugar and garlic. Blend for 1 minute. To assemble the salad, place the crispy vermicelli in equal portions on 4 plates. Pour the dressing over the salad, toss and arrange portions of the salad over the vermicelli. Serves 4.

Five Spice Deep-Fried Chicken

3-4 lb. frying chicken, cut into
  pieces
3 T. Chinese five-spice seasoning
1 t. salt

1/2 t. black pepper
1 T. dried parsley flakes
oil for frying

 Clean the chicken pieces and pat dry with paper towels. Combine the seasoning, salt, pepper and parsley in a small bowl. Lift the skin from each piece of chicken, keep the skin intact, and rub the spices under the skin. Replace the skin on each piece. Heat the deep fryer to 355°F according to the manufacturer's instructions. Fry 1-2 pieces of chicken at a time for 15-20 minutes, turning once. When done, the chicken will be golden brown and cooked through completely. Drain on absorbent paper and repeat with the remaining chicken. Serves 4.

Chicken Pomodoro with Angel Hair Pasta

4 chicken breast halves
1 c. flour
1 t. salt
1/2 t. black pepper
1/2 t. dried Italian seasoning
2 T. olive oil
1/2 c. chicken broth
2 T. dry white wine

1/2 c. tomatoes, chopped
1 T. garlic, finely minced
2 T. fresh parsley, minced
2 T. heavy cream
8 oz. angel hair pasta, cooked al dente and drained
2 T. green onions, thinly sliced
oil for frying

 Place the chicken breast pieces between 2 pieces of plastic wrap and pound with a meat mallet until ¼-inch thick. Combine the flour, salt, pepper and Italian seasoning. Coat the chicken in the flour mixture. Heat the deep fryer to 355°F according to the manufacturer's instructions. Fry each cutlet in the oil for 4-5 minutes, or until crispy brown and cooked through. Drain on absorbent paper and keep warm in the oven.

Prepare the sauce by combining the chicken broth and white wine over medium heat. Stir and add the tomatoes, garlic and parsley. Cook for 1 minute. Add the heavy cream and mix just until smooth. Divide the angel hair pasta among 4 plates, top with the chicken breasts and pour the cream sauce evenly over all. Garnish with the green onions. Serves 4.

Spanish Tapas Potatoes

4 russet potatoes, peeled and cut into 1/2-inch cubes

14 oz. can diced tomatoes, drained

4 cloves garlic, finely minced

1/4 t. sugar

1/4 t. chili powder

2 T. chili sauce

oil for frying

 Heat the deep fryer to 375°F according to the manufacturer's instructions. Fry the potatoes a handful at a time for 3-4 minutes or until cooked through and brown. Drain on absorbent paper. In a medium sauté pan, combine the tomatoes, garlic, sugar, chili powder and chili sauce. Heat just to simmer. Add the potatoes and gently toss. Serve immediately. Serves 4.

East Indian Samosas

Samosas Vegetable Filling

1 T. vegetable oil

1 c. green cabbage, shredded

1 c. frozen peas, thawed and
drained

1/2 c. sweet onion, chopped

2 T. green chilies, diced

1 t. fresh ginger, minced

1/4 c. fresh mint leaves, minced

1/4 c. fresh cilantro leaves,
minced

1/2 t. salt

1/2 t. black pepper

3 russet potatoes, mashed

Samosas Dough

2 c. flour

1/4 c. butter or margarine, melted

1 t. salt

1/4 c. water (or as needed)

oil for frying

 In a large sauté pan, heat the oil until hot, but not smoking. Add the cabbage and peas. Lower the heat slightly and add the onions. Cook for 2 minutes. Add the green chilies, ginger, mint, cilantro, salt and pepper and mix well. Add the mashed potatoes and mix again. Cook for 1 minute over low heat. Set aside.

To prepare the Samosas Dough, combine the flour, butter and salt in a large bowl. Mix well. Add the water, a tablespoon at a time, until the dough leaves the sides of the bowl and is fairly well-incorporated. Turn onto a lightly floured board and knead the dough for 5 minutes. Cut the dough into balls the size of large walnuts. Roll each ball to a 6-inch circle. Place 1 large tablespoon of filling on half of each circle and fold the dough over the remaining half. Seal the edges of each semi-circle with water and crimp with a fork.

Heat the deep fryer to 355°F according to the manufacturer's instructions. Fry 4-5 samosas for 4-5 minutes, or until brown and heated through. Turn once during frying. Drain on absorbent paper and repeat with the remaining samosas. Serve with chutney or condiments of your choice. Serves 6.

CHAPTER SEVEN

Breads, Hush Puppies & More

There are a number of breads that can be prepared in your deep fryer and they are all absolutely delicious! The quick-cooking method of the fryer gives the crust a golden brown and crispy texture, which adds to the inviting experience of tasting a warm, fresh piece of bread.

Add a bit of variety to your meals by including one of these breads any night of the week. If you are grilling a simple cut of meat or seafood, use our *Golden Cheese Toast* as a flavorful accompaniment. If you are entertaining and would like to add an exotic flair to your meal, don't miss the *Moroccan Pita Crisps with Black Olive Tapenade*. And, when you are creating family meals that call for bread, turn to the *Navajo Fry Bread* or *Fried Italian Bread* to please everyone's appetite in a flash.

In addition to these recipes, you may want to experiment with your own favorite breads using your deep fryer. Almost every culture in the world uses bread as a foundational element of the daily diet, so you'll find that it's fun and easy to adapt many recipes to cooking in the deep fryer. Try creating sweet bread, batter breads and other specialties that you would normally bake in your oven. Your new favorite recipe may be just around the corner!

Navajo Fry Bread

21/4 c. flour

2 t. baking powder

1 t. salt

3/4 c. warm water

yellow cornmeal

oil for frying

 In a large bowl, combine the flour, baking powder, salt and water. Thoroughly mix until the dough leaves the sides of the bowl. Add water, if needed to process the dough into a smooth dough. Pull small balls from the dough (about the shape of a walnut) and place on a board that has been lightly dusted with cornmeal. Roll each ball to 1/4-inch thickness. With your thumb, press a hole in the center of each piece of bread.

Heat the deep fryer to 375°F according to the manufacturer's instructions. Fry 1-2 pieces of bread for 2-3 minutes, turning once. The bread will be golden brown and cooked through completely when done. Drain on absorbent paper and dust with powdered sugar or jam to serve. Makes about 12.

Fried Italian Bread

1 large prepared pizza crust (such as Boboli®) oil for frying	balsamic vinegar and olive oil to taste

 Heat the deep fryer to 355°F according to the manufacturer's instructions. Cut the pizza crust in strips 2 inches wide and 2 inches long. Place 3-4 pieces of crust in the fryer and cook for 2 minutes. Place each crust on absorbent paper repeat with the remaining crust. Serves 6 as an accompaniment to the entrée.

Golden Cheese Toast

1/2 c. Romano cheese, grated	salt and pepper to taste
2 T. flour	12 slices sourdough bread, 1/2-inch thick
pinch cayenne pepper	
1/2 t. paprika	2 eggs, beaten
	oil for frying

 In a large shallow dish, combine the cheese, flour, cayenne pepper, paprika, salt and pepper. Toss to blend well. Heat the deep fryer to 375°F according to the manufacturer's instructions. Dip 1 piece of bread in the egg and pat lightly in the cheese and flour mixture, turning once to coat. Fry 1 piece of bread for 3 minutes, or until golden brown and crispy. Drain on absorbent paper and repeat with the remaining slices. Serves 6.

Moroccan Pita Crisps with Black Olive Tapenade

6 6-inch pita breads	**Black Olive Tapenade:**
1/4 c. olive oil	3/4 c. black olives, chopped
oil for frying	2 T. dairy sour cream
	1 green onion, thinly sliced
	1/4 t. salt
	1/4 t. black pepper, freshly ground

Slice each pita in half and split open completely so that there are four quarters. Cut each quarter in half again. Heat the deep fryer to 375°F according to the manufacturer's instructions. Fry 2-4 pieces of pita bread for 2 minutes and drain on absorbent paper. Repeat with the remaining pita bread.

To prepare the *Black Olive Tapenade*, place the olives, sour cream, green onion, salt and pepper in a blender and pulse for 5-10 seconds. Spread each pita crisp with the tapenade as desired. Serves 6 as an accompaniment or appetizer.

Cheddar Cheese Hush Puppies

2 c. cheddar cheese, shredded	1 t. salt
1/2 c. flour	2 eggs, beaten
1/2 c. yellow cornmeal	1 c. milk
1 t. baking powder	oil for frying
1/2 t. baking soda	

In a large mixing bowl, combine the cheese, flour, cornmeal, baking powder, baking soda and salt. Mix well. Add the eggs and milk and mix again. Heat the deep fryer to 340°F according to the manufacturer's instructions. Place 4-5 spoonfuls of dough into the deep fryer. Fry for 2-3 minutes, or until golden brown and cooked throughout. Drain on absorbent paper and repeat with the remaining batter. Makes approximately 3 dozen hush puppies.

Homemade Gourmet Salad & Soup Croutons

6 slices day-old bread of your
   choice
1/2 t. ground oregano
1/2 t. garlic salt

1/4 t. celery salt
1/2 t. black pepper
oil for frying

 Remove the crusts from the bread and cut into 1/2-inch squares. Combine the oregano, garlic salt, celery salt and pepper in a small bowl. Heat the deep fryer to 375°F according to the manufacturer's instructions. Place 8-10 crouton squares in the oil and fry for 2 minutes, turning once to brown evenly. Drain on absorbent paper and repeat with the remaining croutons. While warm, dust the croutons with the seasonings. Use the croutons with your favorite salads or soups. Store croutons in an air-tight bag for up to 4 days. Makes about 4 cups of croutons.

Cajun Hush Puppies

1 c. yellow cornmeal	1/2 t. baking soda
1/2 c. flour	2 T. vegetable oil
1/4 t. cayenne pepper	1/2 c. buttermilk
1/4 t. Cajun seasoning	2 eggs, beaten
1/2 t. salt	oil for frying

 In a large bowl, combine the cornmeal, flour, cayenne pepper, Cajun seasoning, salt and soda. Blend well. Add the 2 T. vegetable oil, buttermilk and eggs and blend until the batter is very smooth. Heat the deep fryer to 355°F according to the manufacturer's instructions. Place 4-5 spoonfuls of batter in the deep fryer. Fry for 2-3 minutes, turning once, or until golden brown and cooked through. Drain on absorbent paper and repeat with the remaining batter. Makes about 24 hush puppies.

Ranch Style Fried Bagel Chips

6 bagels, sliced into 1/4-inch thick pieces

2 oz. pkg. ranch salad dressing mix

1/2 c. extra virgin olive oil

freshly ground black pepper

oil for frying

Heat the deep fryer to 375°F according to the manufacturer's instructions. Place 2-3 slices of bagel in the deep fryer and fry for 2 minutes, turning once. Remove and drain on absorbent paper. Repeat with the remaining bagel slices. While the bagels are cooling, mix together in a small bowl, the salad dressing mix, olive oil and black pepper. Stir well. Using a pastry brush, cover 1 side of each bagel chip with the oil/dressing mix and allow to stand for 30 minutes. Serve immediately or store in an air-tight container. Makes about 24 large bagel chips.

Fresh Herbed Drop Biscuits

2 c. flour	1/2 t. fresh thyme, finely minced
1/2 c. butter or margarine, softened	1/2 t. fresh rosemary, finely minced
1 c. buttermilk	2 t. baking powder
1 t. fresh parsley, finely minced	1 t. salt
1/2 t. fresh oregano, finely minced	oil for frying

 Heat the deep fryer to 340°F according to the manufacturer's instructions. Cut the butter into the flour using a pastry cutter or two knives. Add the buttermilk and blend. Add the parsley, oregano, thyme, rosemary, baking powder and salt and mix for 2 minutes by hand. Carefully drop 3-4 well-rounded tablespoons of dough into the deep fryer and fry for 3-4 minutes, turning once. Remove the biscuits and drain on absorbent paper. Repeat with the remaining biscuits. Serves 4.

Butter-Brushed Fried Rolls

2 1/4 oz. pkgs. active dry yeast	1 t. salt
1/2 c. warm water (110°-115°F)	4-5 c. flour
3/4 c. milk	2 eggs, beaten
1/2 c. shortening	1/4 c. butter, melted
1/2 c. sugar	oil for frying

 In a large mixing bowl, combine the dry yeast and the water. Stir to dissolve completely. Add the milk, shortening, sugar and salt and beat with the electric mixer for 2 minutes. Add 2 cups of the flour and beat again until smooth. Gradually add more flour until the dough leaves the sides of the bowl. Turn the dough onto a lightly floured board and knead for 5-10 minutes, or until smooth and elastic. Place the dough in a bowl that has been lighted greased and turn the dough. Cover with a clean cloth and allow to rise for 1½-2 hours.

Punch down the dough and pull the dough into small balls about the size of large walnuts. Place the rolls on a large tray and allow to rise again, about 45 minutes. Heat the deep fryer to 355°F according to the manufacturer's instructions. Place 2-3 rolls in the deep fryer and fry for 4-5 minutes, or until golden brown and cooked through. Remove and drain on absorbent paper. Lightly brush with the melted butter. Repeat with the remaining rolls. Makes about 26 rolls.

Southern Fried Spoon Bread

2 eggs	1 c. canned creamed corn
8 1/2 oz. pkg. corn muffin mix	1/2 c. dairy sour cream
1 c. canned whole kernel corn, drained	1 c. Swiss cheese, shredded
	oil for frying

 In a large bowl, combine the eggs, corn muffin mix, whole corn, creamed corn, sour cream and cheese. Mix thoroughly. Heat the deep fryer to 355°F according to the manufacturer's instructions. Drop the batter by tablespoons into the oil, frying 3-4 pieces at a time. Fry for 3 minutes, turn, and fry for an additional 1-2 minutes, or until the bread is golden brown and cooked through. Drain on absorbent paper and repeat with the remaining batter. Serves 6.

Onion & Dill Hush Puppies

1 c. flour	1 t. fresh parsley, finely minced
1 c. yellow cornmeal	1 egg
4 t. baking powder	3/4 c. buttermilk
1 t. salt	1/4 c. white onion, finely minced
1 t. fresh dill, finely minced	oil for frying

 In a large mixing bowl, combine the flour, cornmeal, baking powder, salt, dill and parsley. Mix to blend. Add the egg, buttermilk and onion and mix again for about 2 minutes to make a batter. Heat the deep fryer to 355°F according to the manufacturer's instructions. Place 4-5 spoonfuls of batter in the deep fryer. Fry for 2-3 minutes, turning once, or until golden brown and cooked through. Drain on absorbent paper and repeat with the remaining batter. Makes about 24 hush puppies.

Mexican Sopaipillas

2 c. flour	1/8 c. shortening
1 t. salt	2/3 c. warm water
1 t. sugar	oil for frying

 In a medium bowl, mix together the flour, salt and sugar. Using a pastry cutter or 2 knives, cut the shortening into the flour until the mixture looks like small crumbs. Add the water, 2 tablespoons at a time, tossing with a fork, until the dough leaves the sides of the bowl to form a ball. Place the dough on a lightly floured board and knead 20 times until the dough is smooth. Cover and let rest for 20 minutes. Roll the dough out on a lightly floured board to ⅛-inch thickness and cut into 2-inch squares.

Heat the deep fryer to 355°F according to the manufacturer's instructions. Place 3-4 sopaipillas in the deep fryer and cook for 2-3 minutes, turning once. Remove when the bread is golden brown and cooked through. Drain on absorbent paper and repeat with the remaining sopaipillas. Makes about 40 pieces.

Langos Mini-Breads

2 c. milk

1/2 c. butter or margarine

1/2 c. sugar

2 t. salt

2 1/4 oz. pkgs. active dry yeast

1/2 c. water (110-115°F)

2 eggs, beaten

9 1/2 - 10 c. flour

oil for frying

In a medium saucepan, scald the milk. Cool to lukewarm and add the butter, sugar and salt. Stir well. In a large bowl, sprinkle the yeast over the water and dissolve the yeast completely. Add the milk/butter mixture, the eggs and 5 cups of flour. Use an electric mixer to blend until smooth. Add enough remaining flour to make a soft dough that leaves the sides of the bowl. Turn the dough onto a lightly floured board and knead until smooth, about 5-10 minutes. Coat a large bowl with cooking spray, place the dough in the bowl and turn so that the greased dough is on the top. Cover with a clean cloth and place in a warm area until doubled in size, about 1½ to 2 hours.

Punch down the dough. Pinch off balls about the size of an egg and roll and stretch into a flat circle about ½-inch thick. Pull the dough until it is thin, but not broken. Heat the deep fryer to 375°F according to the manufacturer's instructions. Fry 1-2 breads at a time, for 3-4 minutes, turning once to brown evenly. Drain on absorbent paper and repeat with the remaining breads. Makes about 24 langos mini-breads.

Old-Fashioned Cornmeal Hush Puppies

1 c. flour
1 c. cornmeal
1/2 t. salt
1/2 t. garlic salt

1 egg, beaten
2/3 c. buttermilk (you may substitute milk, if desired)
1/4 c. onion, finely minced
oil for frying

 Combine the flour, cornmeal, salt and garlic salt in a large bowl. Add the egg and buttermilk or milk. Mix well to blend. Add the onion and stir again. Heat the deep fryer to 355°F according to the manufacturer's instructions. Place 4-5 spoonfuls of batter in the deep fryer and cook for 2-3 minutes. Turn once to brown evenly. Drain on absorbent paper and repeat with the remaining batter. Makes about 24 hush puppies.

CHAPTER EIGHT

Delectable Desserts

Deep-fried desserts are truly luscious taste treats! Whether you enjoy fried cookies, fried pies or deep-fried cakes, these delectable desserts are meant to be shared with a warm cup of coffee or tea and family or friends.

The essence of deep-frying desserts is quickly cooking small portions in high heat and dusting or frosting each dessert to create a grand finale. Deep-fried desserts are usually rich, so you'll find that portions are small and often quite delicate. Inside this chapter you will find surprisingly quick-to-fix desserts that are elegant enough to feed guests, such as *Deep-Fried Strawberries with Chocolate Drizzle* and *Grand Marnier® Deep-Fried Peaches*. Favorite family desserts may include *Sweet Pineapple Fritters* and *Deep-Fried Apricot Turnovers*. And, who can resist such delicacies as *Deep-Fried Crispy Ice Cream Balls* and *Fried Cherry Pies*?

Fried Apple Crisps

4 tart apples
2 T. lemon juice
3 T. sugar
1/2 c. flour
1/2 t. salt
1 T. sugar

1/4 c. apple cider
2 eggs, whites and yolks
    separated
1 t. vegetable oil
1/2 c. sugar
1 t. ground cinnamon
oil for frying

 Peel the apples and core. Cut the apples into rings about ¼-inch thick. Place the rings in a medium bowl and cover with the lemon juice and 3 tablespoons of sugar. Toss to coat each ring thoroughly. Set aside. In a large bowl, combine the flour, salt and 1 tablespoon of sugar. Mix well. Add the apple cider and egg yolks, 1 teaspoon of vegetable oil and mix again. In a small, deep bowl, beat until stiff the 2 egg whites and fold them carefully into the batter.

Heat the deep fryer to 375°F according to the manufacturer's instructions. Dip 1 apple ring into the batter and allow the excess to drip back into the bowl. Place in the deep fryer and add 1-2 additional apple rings. Fry for 1 minute, turn and fry for 1-2 minutes or until lightly browned. Remove and drain on absorbent paper. Repeat with the remaining apple rings. Mix together the ½ cup sugar and 1 teaspoon of cinnamon and dust each apple crisp with the mixture. Serve immediately. Makes about 20 apple crisps.

Sweet Pineapple Fritters

1 c. flour
1 t. baking powder
3 T. sugar
1/4 t. ground cinnamon
1/2 t. salt
1/2 c. milk

1 1/2 c. fresh pineapple, cut into small chunks (you may substitute canned, drained pineapple, chopped, if desired)
1 c. powdered sugar
oil for frying

 In a large mixing bowl, combine the flour, baking powder, sugar, cinnamon and salt. Mix well. Add the milk and pineapple and mix again. Heat the deep fryer to 355°F according to the manufacturer's instructions. Place 1 large tablespoon of batter in the fryer and repeat with 2-3 additional tablespoons. Fry for about 3-4 minutes, or until golden and cooked through, turning once. Remove from the fryer and drain on absorbent paper. Dust each fritter with powdered sugar. Repeat with the remaining batter. Makes about 12 fritters.

Deep-Fried Strawberries with Chocolate Drizzle

1 c. prepared baking mix
3/4 c. milk
24 large strawberries, cleaned and dried
oil for frying

Chocolate Drizzle:
4 oz. pkg. chocolate pudding and pie filling
3/4 c. water
3/4 c. light corn syrup
1/4 t. salt
1 t. butter or margarine
1/2 t. vanilla flavoring

 In a medium bowl, combine the baking mix and milk. Blend completely, adding milk if needed to make a smooth batter. Heat the deep fryer to 375°F according to the manufacturer's instructions. Dip the strawberries in the batter, covering completely, and allow the excess batter to drip back into the bowl. Fry 3-4 strawberries at a time for 2-3 minutes. Drain on absorbent paper.

To prepare the *Chocolate Drizzle*, combine the pudding and pie filling mix, the water and the corn syrup in a medium saucepan. Heat until boiling, stirring constantly. Remove from the heat and add the butter and vanilla. Whip until glossy and smooth. Use immediately to drizzle chocolate over each strawberry. Serve immediately. Makes 24 strawberries.

Bow Tie Cookies

10 egg yolks	3 c. flour
1/4 c. sugar	1 t. baking powder
1/4 c. dairy sour cream	1/2 t. salt
1 T. rum	1 c. powdered sugar
1 t. vanilla flavoring	oil for frying

 In a large bowl, beat the egg yolks with the sugar using an electric mixer until very smooth. Add the sour cream, rum and vanilla flavoring and blend again. In a separate bowl, combine the flour, baking powder and salt and gradually add to the batter. Mix until a soft dough forms. Turn the dough onto a lightly floured board and knead for 10 minutes. Add additional flour, if necessary to make a smooth and elastic dough. Divide the dough into quarters. Lightly flour the board again and roll the quarter of dough into a rectangle, 8 inches in length and 16 inches wide. The dough will be very thin and transparent when rolled out completely. Cut the dough into strips about 4 inches in length and 1½ inches wide. Cut a slit in the strip close to one end and pull the long end of the strip through the hole to create a tie.

Heat the deep fryer to 375°F according to the manufacturer's instructions. Place 3-4 cookies in the fryer and cook for 2 minutes, turning once. Drain on absorbent paper and dust with powdered sugar. Makes about 6 dozen cookies.

Grand Marnier® Deep-Fried Peaches

4 ripe whole peaches

2 c. graham cracker crumbs

2 T. sugar

1/4 t. ground cinnamon

1 1/2 c. frozen vanilla bean ice cream

1/2 oz. Grand Marnier® liquor

oil for frying

 Wash the peaches and blanch in boiling water for 30 seconds. Remove from the water and peel the skins from the peaches. Cut the peaches in half and remove the pit. Mix together the crumbs, sugar and cinnamon in a wide, shallow plate. Heat the deep fryer to 375°F according to the manufacturer's instructions. Scoop a large tablespoon of ice cream and pack it inside each peach half. Put the 2 peach halves back together, pressing firmly, and roll the peach in the sugar and cinnamon crumbs. Place 1 peach in the deep fryer for 1-2 minutes, turning once. Remove from the fryer and repeat with the remaining peaches. To serve, drizzle each peach with liquor and light on fire. Serves 4.

Deep-Fried Apricot Turnovers

16 refrigerated croissant rolls
1 c. apricot preserves
2 c. powdered sugar
2 T. milk

pinch of salt
1/2 t. vanilla flavoring
oil for frying

 Place the croissant rolls on a lightly floured board. Carefully overlap 2 triangles slightly on the longest side of each and roll or press together to form 1 square. Place 2 heaping tablespoons of the apricot preserves in the middle of the square and fold over to form a square. Use a fork to crimp the exposed edges of the turnover. Heat the deep fryer to 375°F according to the manufacturer's instructions. Place 1 turnover in the fryer and cook for 3-4 minutes, turning once, until golden brown and cooked through. Drain on absorbent paper and repeat with the remaining turnovers. In a small bowl, mix together the sugar, milk, salt and vanilla flavoring until very smooth. Drizzle the glaze over the turnovers and serve while warm. Makes 8 turnovers.

Homestyle Apple Fritters

1 c. flour
1 t. baking powder
1/2 t. salt
2 eggs, beaten

1/2 c. milk
1 T. vegetable oil
1 c. tart apples, finely chopped
oil for frying

 In a medium bowl, combine the flour, baking powder and salt. Mix well. Add the eggs, milk and oil and blend until very smooth. Add the apples and mix again. Heat the deep fryer to 355°F according to the manufacturer's instructions. Place 3-4 tablespoons of batter into the oil and fry for 3-4 minutes. Turn once while frying. Drain on absorbent paper and dust with powdered sugar, if desired. Makes about 12 fritters.

Oriental Fruit Wonton Cookies

2 c. dried apples, finely chopped
1 c. dried apricots, finely chopped
1 c. brown sugar, packed
1 c. coconut flakes

1/2 c. almonds, finely chopped
24 wonton wrappers
oil for frying

 In a large bowl, combine the apples, apricots, brown sugar, coconut and almonds. Mix well. Place 1 wonton wrapper on a flat surface and scoop 1 large tablespoon of the fruit mixture onto the center of the wrapper. Lightly moisten the edges of the wrapper with water and fold into a triangle. Heat the deep fryer to 355°F according to the manufacturer's instructions. Fry 2-3 wonton at a time for 4-5 minutes, turning once to brown evenly. Drain on absorbent paper and repeat with the remaining cookies. Makes 24 cookies.

Deep-Fried Crispy Ice Cream Balls

1/2 gal. vanilla ice cream
10 c. corn flakes, finely ground
1/4 c. sugar

1 T. ground cinnamon
4 eggs
oil for frying

 Using your hands and an ice cream scoop, press the ice cream into the size of small baseballs and freeze solid for 24 hours. In a medium bowl, combine the corn flakes, sugar and cinnamon and mix well. Place the eggs in a deep bowl and beat well. Dip each ice cream ball in the egg and then roll in the corn flake crumbs. Cover each ball completely with the crumbs. Repeat the egg and crumb dip for each ball. Freeze the balls again for 2 hours.

Heat the deep fryer to 375°F according to the manufacturer's instructions. Working with 1 ice cream ball at a time, place 1 ball in the fryer and fry for 1 minute, or until lightly browned. Remove and place in a bowl. Repeat with the remaining balls and serve immediately. Serves 8.

Deep-Fried Twinkies® Treats

6 Twinkies®
6 wooden ice cream sticks
1 c. milk
2 T. vinegar
1 T. oil

1 c. flour
1 t. baking powder
1/2 t. salt
oil for frying

 Insert the ice cream sticks into the Twinkies lengthwise, leaving 2-3 inches for handles. Freeze the Twinkies for 24 hours. In a large bowl, combine the milk, vinegar, oil, flour, baking powder and salt and blend completely with an electric mixer for 2 minutes. Heat the deep fryer to 375°F according to the manufacturer's instructions. Dip 1 Twinkie in the batter and fry for 3-4 minutes. Use a long-handled spoon to hold the Twinkie down in the oil, if necessary. Drain on absorbent paper and repeat with the remaining Twinkies. Serve immediately. Makes 6 servings.

Fried Cherry Pies

4 c. flour	2 c. canned cherry pie filling
1 t. salt	2 c. powdered sugar
2 t. baking powder	1/4 c. milk
1 c. shortening	1 t. vanilla flavoring
1 c. milk	oil for frying

 In a medium bowl, combine the flour, salt and baking powder. Mix well. Using a pastry cutter or 2 knives, add the shortening and mix until the pastry resembles small crumbs. Add the milk, ¼ cup at a time, until the pastry is soft and leaves the sides of the bowl. Form into a ball. Divide the dough into 20 small balls. On a lightly floured board, roll 1 ball into a circle about 4-inches wide. Place 2 tablespoons of cherry pie filling on the dough. Lightly moisten the edges of the circle with water and fold in half, sealing the edges. Crimp the edges with a fork.

Heat the deep fryer to 375°F according to the manufacturer's instructions. Place 2-3 pies in the fryer and cook for 4 minutes. Turn and cook for 3-4 minutes, or until the pies are golden brown and cooked through. Drain on absorbent paper and repeat with the remaining pies. To prepare the glaze, mix the powdered sugar, milk and vanilla in a small bowl until blended. Drizzle over each pie and serve while warm. Makes about 20 pies.

Fresh Pear & Pecan Fritters

2 c. fresh pears, cored and cut
  into small cubes

1/2 c. pecans, chopped

1 1/2 c. flour

1 t. baking powder

1/4 c. sugar

1/4 t. ground cinnamon

1/4 t. ground nutmeg

1/2 t. salt

3/4 c. milk

1 c. powdered sugar

oil for frying

 In a large bowl, combine the pears, pecans, flour, baking powder, sugar, cinnamon, nutmeg and salt. Add the milk and mix well. Heat the deep fryer to 355°F according to the manufacturer's instructions. Place 1 large tablespoon of batter in the fryer and add 2-3 additional tablespoons, as space allows. Fry for 3-4 minutes, or until cooked through and lightly browned. Drain on absorbent paper and dust with powdered sugar. Repeat with the remaining batter. Makes about 12 fritters.

Cinnamon & Spice Funnel Cakes

1 1/2 c. flour	1/4 t. ground cloves
1 t. baking powder	2 eggs, beaten
1/4 t. salt	1 1/2 c. milk
1/4 t. ground cinnamon	2 T. sugar
1/4 t. ground nutmeg	oil for frying

 Combine in a large bowl the flour, baking powder, salt, cinnamon, nutmeg and cloves. Add the eggs, milk and sugar and mix until the batter is very smooth. Heat the deep fryer to 375°F according to the manufacturer's instructions. Using a small funnel, place 1 finger over the small hole and fill the funnel to within ½-inch of the top. Placing the funnel over the hot oil, remove your finger and allow the batter to pour into the oil, making a circular motion with the batter. Fry for 1 minute, turn and fry for 1-2 minutes, or until golden and cooked through. Drain on absorbent paper and repeat with the remaining batter. Makes about 8 funnel cakes.

Fresh Raspberry Fritters with Sour Cream Sauce

1 c. flour	**Sour Cream Sauce**
1 t. baking powder	1 c. dairy sour cream
1 T. sugar	1/2 c. cream cheese, softened
1/2 t. salt	1 T. sugar
2 eggs, yolks and whites separated	2 t. lemon juice
1/2 c. milk	
1 c. fresh raspberries, rinsed and dried	
oil for frying	

 Combine the flour, baking powder, sugar and salt in a medium bowl. Add the egg yolks and milk. Beat the egg whites until stiff and fold into the batter. Gently fold the raspberries into the batter. Heat the deep fryer to 375°F according to the manufacturer's instructions. Spoon 1 large tablespoon of batter into the fryer and add 2-3 additional spoonfuls. Fry for 3-4 minutes, turning once. Drain on absorbent paper and repeat with the remaining batter. To make the *Sour Cream*

Sauce, use an electric mixer or blender to whip together the sour cream, cream cheese, sugar and lemon juice. To serve, drizzle the sauce over the each fritter and serve immediately. Makes about 12 fritters.

Deep-Fried Cheese & Citrus Cannoli

2 c. flour
1 T. sugar
1/4 t. ground cinnamon
1 egg, beaten
1/2 c. Marsala wine
1 t. vanilla flavoring
oil for frying

Cheese & Citrus Filling:
1 lb. ricotta cheese, drained
1/4 c. mascarpone cheese
1 c. powdered sugar, sifted
1/4 t. ground cinnamon
1 t. vanilla flavoring
2 T. orange extract or flavoring
1/2 c. mini semi-sweet chocolate chips

Mix together in a large bowl the flour, sugar and cinnamon. Mix in the egg, wine and vanilla flavoring. Blend well. Turn the dough onto a lightly floured board and knead for 15 minutes. The dough should be smooth and satiny when ready. Cover and let stand for 2 hours. Roll the dough into a very thin sheet (about ⅛-inch thick). Cut the dough into circles 5 inches in diameter. Wrap the dough circles into metal cannoli forms. Fold the dough around each form loosely. Seal the edges of the dough with the beaten egg white and press tightly.

Heat the deep fryer to 375°F according to the manufacturer's instructions. Fry 1-2 cannoli at a time for 3-4 minutes or until golden brown. Drain the cannoli on absorbent paper and cool.

To make the *Cheese & Citrus Filling,* use an electric mixer or blender to combine the cheeses, sugar, cinnamon, vanilla and orange flavoring. Blend for 1 minute at high speed. Remove the beaters and fold in the chocolate chips evenly. Fill each cannoli form with the cheese filling and serve or refrigerate until servings. Garnish with orange slices, if desired. Makes 12 cannoli.